STUDY GUIDE TO ACCOMPANY

PROFESSIONAL
COOKING

ISBN: 0-471-08931-1

Printed in the United States of America

10 9 8 7 6 5 4 3 2

TO THE STUDENT

This *Study Guide* is a companion to *Professional Cooking*, third edition. Its purpose is to help you study and review the material in the text.

Learning to cook is primarily a practical, hands-on endeavor. It is, for the most part, a matter of learning manual skills by practicing them under the guidance of an instructor or supervisor, and then improving those skills by repeated practice.

These practical skills, however, depend on a large body of knowledge and understanding. You need to know about cooking theory, basic procedures, general guidelines, and ingredient information. Using this manual will help you to study and to master this material.

This *Study Guide* is arranged by chapter, corresponding to the 30 chapters in *Professional Cooking*. Each chapter contains several exercises that you can use to test your own knowledge. Then you can see what you have learned and what you need to review. The following are guidelines for using the different kinds of exercises.

Chapter Goals

These are the same goals that appear at the beginning of each text chapter. They are not exercises, but they are included here as a reminder of the specific skills you should be learning in each chapter.

Terms

The first exercise in each chapter is a list of definitions or descriptions of terms used in the kitchen. In each of the blanks provided, write the term that is defined or described. (In Chapter 3, some of the questions in the terms section ask you to identify a picture; give the name of the item in the illustration. You will find more questions asking you to identify pictures in some other chapters.)

This is the only kind of exercise you will find in every chapter. Why is there so much emphasis on terms? It is important not only that you learn how to cook but that you can communicate with other cooks. A food service career involves teamwork and sharing of information. To communicate, you must know the language of the kitchen.

True/False Questions

For each question, draw a circle around the T if the statement is completely true. Draw a circle around the F if the statement is only partly true or is completely false.

Completion, Short-Answer Questions, and Other Written Exercises

Many exercises ask you to fill in blanks with words or phrases or to write out various kinds of answers.

If the problem is a straight question, a space is provided for you to write out the answer.

If the problem is a statement that contains one or more blanks, fill in the blanks so that the statement is true and makes a complete sentence.

If the problem asks you to write a procedure or to explain how to do a task, write out the procedure using numbered steps. You do not need to *explain* each step, the way the text sometimes does, but be sure that your procedure is complete. Don't leave out any steps.

Math Exercises

Math is very important in the professional kitchen. Throughout your career you will have to make many kinds of mathematical calculations. Some of the most basic of these are explained in *Professional Cooking*.

In Chapter 5, you learn how to do the following kinds of math:

Handling units of measure
Working with food cost percentages
Performing yield tests
Converting recipe yields
Calculating portion costs

The last two of these are so important that you will find exercises throughout this manual to give you practice.

Other kinds of math problems are explained in Chapters 16 and 24. Whenever you have difficulty with any of the math problems, turn to the explanation in the text and review it.

Note that math exercises using units of measure appear twice, once with U.S. units and once with metric units. Complete whichever exercises your instructor asks you to do.

These are the kinds of exercises you will find most often in this manual. There are also other kinds of problems and questions that are especially included to help you review the material in a particular chapter. The instructions at the beginning of each of these sections explain how to do the problems.

acquire skills in selecting, from among the equipment, utensils, and tools available in a commercial kitchen, the implements appropriate to particular food preparation tasks
- acquire knowledge and understanding about the Public Health Act
- lop and demonstrate safe personal work habits
- learn about career opportunities and training in the food industry
- become involved in co-operative education placement in the food service industry
- qualify for credit towards an apprenticeship through the Linkage program

Course Overview

There are 13 units in this course:

1. Tools and Equipment
2. Sanitation, food-borne diseases, personal hygiene, food storage, handling and preparation, cleaning & sanitizing equipment
3. Safety, preventing cuts, burns, fires, injuries from machines and equipment, falls, strains and injuries from lifting
4. Pre-Preparation, planning & organizing for pre-preparation, preparation for set meal service, and extended meal service
5. Cooking Meats, roasting, baking, broiling, grilling, pan-broiling, and sautéing, pan-frying, griddling, simmering, and braising.
6. Understanding Poultry, composition, structure, inspection & grading, classification & market form, handling & storage
7. Cooking Poultry, roasting, baking, broiling, grilling, pan-broiling, and sautéing, pan-frying, griddling, simmering, and braising.
8. Understanding fish, composition, and structure, special problems in cooking fish, varieties & characteristics.
9. Cooking Fish, baking, broiling, pan-broiling, sautéing, pan-frying, girdling, and poaching.
10. Understanding Vegetables, controlling (texture change, flavor change, color change, nutrient losses.
11. Cooking Vegetables, baking, broiling, grilling, pan-broiling, sautéing, pan-frying, girdling, simmering, and braising.
12. Potatoes and other starches, cooking potatoes, cooking rice, variety of potatoes, and rice, variety of recipe available.
13. Salads and Salad Dressings, types of salads, ingredients, arrangement and presentation, recipes & techniques.

Unit one: Tools and Equipment (.25 week)
Unit two: Sanitation, food-borne diseases, personal hygiene, food storage, handling and preparation, cleaning & sanitizing equipment (2 weeks)
Unit three: Safety, preventing cuts, burns, fires, injuries from machines and equipment, falls, strains and injuries from lifting. (1 weeks)
Unit four: Pre-Preparation, planning & organizing for pre-preparation, preparation for set meal service, and extended meal service. (2 weeks)
Unit five: Cooking Meats, roasting, baking, broiling, grilling, pan-broiling, sautéing, pan-frying, girdling, simmering, and braising. (2 weeks)
Unit six: Understanding Poultry, composition, structure, inspection & grading, classification & market form, handling & storage. (1 weeks)
Unit seven: Cooking Poultry, roasting, baking, broiling, grilling, pan-broiling, sautéing, pan-frying, simmering, and braising. (2 weeks)
Unit eight: Understanding fish, composition, structure, special problems in cooking fish, varieties & characteristics. (1 weeks)
Unit nine: Cooking Fish, baking, broiling, pan-broiling, sautéing, pan-frying, girdling, and poaching. (1 weeks)
Unit ten: Understanding Vegetables, controlling (texture change, flavor change, color change, nutrient losses. (.5 week)
Unit eleven: Cooking Vegetables, baking, broiling, grilling, pan-broiling, sautéing, pan-frying, girdling, simmering, and braising. (1 week)
Unit twelve: Potatoes and other starches, cooking potatoes, cooking rice, variety of potatoes, and rice, variety of recipe available. (1 week)
Unit thirteen: Salads and Salad Dressings, types of salads, ingredients, arrangement and presentation, recipes & techniques. (.25 weeks)

Assignments and Student Evaluation

The extent to which the objectives of the course have been realized will be determined by:

- The monthly completion of the assigned chapters in the study book.

- The successful completion of the monthly test on the contents of the chapters in the study book.

The successful completion of the final exam in food service theory.

CONTENTS

THE FOOD SERVICE INDUSTRY

This chapter gives you a general picture of modern food service and a brief look at the history of the profession. The chapter is short, and there is not much technical information that you have to memorize, but there are some important concepts that you should be familiar with. These questions will help you review.

After studying Chapter 1, you should be able to:

1. Discuss the development of modern food service, including the effects of recent food and equipment technology.
2. Identify the major stations in a classical kitchen.
3. Discuss the factors that influence the organization of modern kitchens.
4. Work in a professional manner.

A. Terms

Fill in each blank with the term that is defined or described.

_____ 1. The person in charge of the kitchen.

_____ 2. The person responsible for preparing cold foods, such as salads, salad dressings, and cold hors d'oeuvres.

_____ 3. French term for a new style of cooking, developed mainly in the 1970s, especially popular in France.

_____ 4. The chef who is sometimes known as the father of twentieth-century cooking, and considered the greatest chef of his age (he died in 1935).

_____ 5. The person responsible for preparing vegetables, starches, soups, and eggs.

_____ 6. The person responsible for preparing sauces, sautéed foods, and stews.

_____ **7.** The person who replaces other station chefs when they are absent.

_____ **8.** The French chef who is considered the greatest chef of the early nineteenth century; he refined and organized cooking, and he was also famous for creating elaborate display pieces.

_____ **9.** The person responsible for preparing roasted and braised meats.

_____ **10.** The person responsible for preparing desserts and pastries.

_____ **11.** In a large establishment, the person who is responsible for all aspects of food production, including menu planning, purchasing, costing, and planning work schedules; in other words, the manager of a large kitchen.

_____ **12.** The person who reports to the person described in number 11, and who directly manages the kitchen production staff.

_____ **13.** The person who is in charge of the kitchen and who also works at one or more of the production stations, usually in smaller establishments.

_____ **14.** A person who is in charge of one particular area of production in a kitchen.

_____ **15.** A set of attitudes and code of behavior followed by successful food service workers.

B. Matching

Column 1 below lists some of the items prepared by the kitchen of a certain hotel. Column 2 lists the titles of the station cooks. In the blanks provided before each food item, write the letter from column 2 which corresponds to the title of the cook who prepares it.

_____ **1.** Roast beef top round   **a.** Saucier

_____ **2.** White wine sauce   **b.** Entremetier

_____ **3.** Chocolate cream pie   **c.** Rotisseur

_____ **4.** Trout amandine   **d.** Garde Manger

_____ **5.** Broiled veal chops   **e.** Grillardin

_____ **6.** Waldorf salad   **f.** Poissonier

_____ **7.** Braised veal shoulder   **g.** Patissier

_____ **8.** Lamb stew

_____ **9.** Canapés

_____ **10.** Blue cheese dressing

_____ **11.** Boiled potatoes

_____ **12.** Roast chicken with gravy

_____ **13.** Split pea soup

_____ **14.** Fried breaded shrimp

_____ **15.** Beef stew

_____ **16.** Chicken liver pâté

_____ **17.** Baked apples

_____ **18.** Sautéed veal scaloppine

_____ **19.** Steamed broccoli

_____ **20.** Poached halibut steaks

C. True/False

T   F   **1.** The position of short-order cook is an entry-level job, because it requires no skills or experience.

T   F   **2.** Institutional kitchens like school cafeterias usually do more cooking to order than restaurants do.

T   F   **3.** Because modern technology uses so many new chemicals, food poisoning is more of a danger today than it was a hundred years ago.

T   F   **4.** The word *chef* is a French term meaning *cook*.

T   F   **5.** Because more and more people are beginning to appreciate fresh foods, convenience foods are becoming less important in food service kitchens.

T   F   **6.** Teamwork is not important in a restaurant where most dishes are cooked to order, because each cook completes his or her own specific tasks.

T   F   **7.** Good restaurants have high menu prices, because high-quality food always costs more to prepare than poor or average food.

T   F   **8.** The *tournant* is the cook who is responsible for preparing foods on a rotisserie.

T   F   **9.** The organization of the kitchen staff depends in part on whether foods are mostly cooked to order or mostly prepared ahead in large quantities.

T   F   **10.** Because of the new styles of cooking developed in the past 25 years, the old techniques of the so-called "classical cooking" are no longer used.

SANITATION AND SAFETY

Good sanitation and safety practices must underlie all your work as a food service professional. The exercises in this chapter help to reinforce your understanding of sanitation and food-borne diseases, especially because sanitation is the subject of many laws and regulations governing this industry.

After studying Chapter 2, you should be able to:

1. Prevent food poisoning and food-borne diseases by exercising proper hygiene, food handling and storage techniques, cleaning and sanitizing procedures and pest control.
2. Develop safe work habits to prevent injuries and avoid common hazards in the kitchen.

A. Terms

Fill in each blank with the term that is defined or described.

_____ 1. A food-borne disease caused by a parasite sometimes found in undercooked pork.

_____ 2. Any bacteria that can cause disease.

_____ 3. Any food-borne disease caused by toxins or poisons that are produced by bacteria while they are growing in food.

_____ 4. Any food-borne disease caused by organisms that get into the intestinal system and attack the body.

_____ 5. A term that describes bacteria that grow when no air is present.

_____ 6. The name for the temperature range in which disease-causing bacteria will grow easily.

_____ 7. A term that describes bacteria that need air to grow.

_____ **8.** The period of time after bacteria come in contact with a food and before they start growing and multiplying.

_____ **9.** A general term for diseases caused by such substances as lead, cyanide, and copper.

_____ **10.** Removing visible soil.

_____ **11.** Killing disease-causing bacteria.

_____ **12.** The transfer of disease-causing bacteria to food from another food or from equipment or work surfaces.

_____ **13.** The movement of food through a food service operation.

_____ **14.** A food safety system usually known by the initials HACCP. (Write out the five-word name.)

_____

_____

_____

_____ **15.** A risk that can lead to a dangerous condition in food; a term used in the system described in number 14.

_____ **16.** An action that can be taken to eliminate or minimize a risk as described in number 15.

B. Review of Food-Borne Diseases

Fill in the blanks as required.

1. *Botulism*

　a. Caused by what organism? _____

　b. What foods might carry it? _____

　　_____

　c. How can it be prevented? _____

　　_____

　　_____

2. *Staph poisoning*

    a. Caused by what organism? _____

    b. What foods might carry it? _____

    _____

    _____

    c. How can it be prevented? _____

    _____

    _____

3. *Salmonella*

    a. Caused by what organism? _____

    b. What foods might carry it? _____

    _____

    _____

    c. How can it be prevented? _____

    _____

    _____

4. *Clostridium perfringens*

    a. Where do the disease-causing bacteria come from? _____

    _____

    b. What foods might carry the bacteria? _____

    _____

    _____

    c. How can the disease be prevented? _____

    _____

    _____

5. *Strep infection*

    a. Where do the disease-causing bacteria come from? _____

    _____

    b. What foods might carry the bacteria? _____

    _____

    _____

    c. How can the disease be prevented? _____

    _____

    _____

6. *Infectious hepatitis*

    a. Where do the disease-causing organisms come from? _____

    _____

    b. How can the disease be prevented? _____

    _____

7. *Trichinosis*

    a. Where do the disease-causing organisms come from? _____

    _____

    b. How can the disease be prevented? _____

    _____

8. *Escherichia coli*

    a. Where do the disease-causing bacteria come from? _____

    _____

    b. What foods might carry the bacteria? _____

    _____

    _____

    c. How can the disease be prevented? _____

    _____

    _____

C. Short-Answer Questions

1. What are the three basic ways to control bacteria that cause food-borne disease? _____
   _____
   _____

2. How are most food-borne disease bacteria spread? _____
   _____

3. What are the two purposes of safe food storage? _____
   _____
   _____

4. Give three examples of times when food workers must wash their hands _____
   _____
   _____

5. Perishable foods must be held or stored at a temperature lower than _____ or higher than
   _____

6. What is the recommended temperature for freezer storage? _____

7. Pork products should be cooked to an internal temperature of _____.

8. What are the four basic methods of controlling insect and rodent infestations? _____
   _____
   _____
   _____

9. What type of fire extinguisher do you need to put out a grease fire? _____

10. What is meant by the expression "building safety into the worker"? _____
    _____
    _____
    _____

11. Discuss how the flow of food is considered when setting up a system for food safety. _____

_____

_____

_____

_____

_____

12. What three categories of hazards can result in food becoming dangerous to eat? _____

_____

_____

TOOLS AND EQUIPMENT

You might think of this chapter as a guide to the professional kitchen or as a catalog of basic equipment. The following exercises help you review your understanding of the tools you will be working with.

After studying Chapter 3, you should be able to:

Understand the safe and efficient use of standard kitchen equipment.

A. Terms

For each of the first 10 questions, fill in the blank with the term that is described or defined. For questions 11 through 30, write the name of the items pictured and their most important uses in the blanks provided.

_____ 1. A type of oven that uses burning wood to provide smoke or heat or both.

_____ 2. Another name for a hot-water bath.

_____ 3. The most widely used metal for pots and pans used in restaurants.

_____ 4. An attachment for mixers and food choppers, used to cut foods into cube shapes.

_____ 5. A steam-jacketed kettle that can be tilted for emptying.

_____ 6. A mixer attachment used to mix and develop yeast doughs.

_____ 7. A flat, smooth, metal surface on which food is cooked directly, such as pancakes, eggs, and hamburgers.

_____ 8. The portion of the metal knife blade that is inside the handle.

_____ 9. A sword-shaped tool used to true the edges of knives.

_____ 10. An item that cooks foods by turning them on spits in front of heating elements.

11.

Name of item: _____

Major use: _____

_____

12.

Name of item: _____

Major use: _____

_____

13.

Name of item: _____

Major use: _____

_____

14.

Name of item: _____

Major use: _____

_____

15.

Name of item: _____

Major use: _____

_____

16.

Name of item: _____

Major use: _____

_____

17.

Name of item: _____

Major use: _____

_____

18.

Name of item: _____

Major use: _____

_____

19.

Name of item: _____

Major use: _____

_____

20.

Name of item: _____

Major use: _____

_____

21.

Name of item: _____

Major use: _____

_____

22.

Name of item: _____

Major use: _____

_____

23.

Name of item: _____

Major use: _____

_____

24.

Name of item: _____

Major use: _____

_____

25.

Name of item: _____

Major use: _____

_____

26.

Name of item: _____

Major use: _____

_____

27.

Name of item: _____

Major use: _____

_____

28.

Name of item: _____

Major use: _____

_____

29.

Name of item: _____

Major use: _____

_____

30.

Name of item: _____

Major use: _____

_____

B. True/False

T F **1.** If an open gas burner doesn't light on first try, it's best to wait a minute before checking the pilot light and trying again.

T F **2.** When filling a fry kettle with fresh solid shortening, it is best to set the thermostat to high (375°F or 190°C) until the fat is melted.

T F **3.** Because of the air circulation in a convection oven, you need to set the temperature higher than for a regular oven.

T F **4.** Pressure steamers must not be opened while the equipment is in operation.

T F **5.** Paddle attachments for mixers are interchangeable and can be used with any size bowl.

T F **6.** Stainless steel is an ideal material for cooking pots because it conducts heat well.

T F **7.** Copper is a good material for pots and pans because it is a good heat conductor, but its disadvantages are that it is heavy and expensive.

T F **8.** The thickness control on a slicing machine should be set at zero when the machine is not in use.

T F **9.** A Number 16 scoop holds about 2 oz (60 g) of food.

T F **10.** Refrigerators operate best when they are as full as possible.

6. True or false: Dry foods heat more quickly in a microwave oven than moist ones do. Explain why or why not.

_____

_____

_____

D. Herb and Spice Reference

It is important to become familiar with the appearance, aroma, and flavor of herbs and spices. Spice charts that describe flavors can be helpful, but there is no substitute for your own experience. Since everyone perceives flavors and aromas differently, a chart that describes herbs and spices in your own words can be your most helpful reference.

This chart may be completed on your own or as assigned by your instructor. Examine each herb or spice just as it is when it comes from its container. Fill in each space by describing your own impressions of its appearance (color and shape), smell, and taste. (The first column can be used to check off those spices assigned by your instructor.) The spaces at the end can be used for additional items not on the list.

√	Product	Appearance	Aroma	Taste
_____	Allspice			
_____	Anise seed			
_____	Basil			
_____	Bay leaf			
_____	Caraway seed			
_____	Cardamom, whole			
_____	Cardamom, ground			

√	Product	Appearance	Aroma	Taste
____	Cayenne or red pepper			
____	Celery seed, whole			
____	Celery salt			
____	Chili powder			
____	Cinnamon, ground			
____	Cinnamon stick			
____	Cloves, ground			
____	Cloves, whole			
____	Coriander seed, whole			
____	Cumin seed, whole			
____	Cumin seed, ground			
____	Curry powder			
____	Fennel seed			
____	Ginger, ground			

√ Product	Appearance	Aroma	Taste
_____ Mace, ground			
_____ Marjoram			
_____ Nutmeg, ground			
_____ Oregano			
_____ Paprika, Hungarian			
_____ Paprika, Spanish			
_____ Pepper, black			
_____ Pepper, white			
_____ Rosemary			
_____ Sage			
_____ Tarragon			
_____ Thyme			

√ Product	Appearance	Aroma	Taste

THE RECIPE: ITS STRUCTURE AND ITS USE

In addition to acquainting you with the structure and functions of written recipes, Chapter 5 introduces the basic elements of kitchen math. In particular, you learn about the following:

1. Handling units of measure
2. Converting recipe yields
3. Making food cost calculations:
   (a) Working with food cost percentages
   (b) Performing yield tests
   (c) Calculating portion costs

Exercises to give you practice in these important calculations are included here. Later chapters contain additional exercises to help you develop these essential skills.

After studying Chapter 5, you should be able to:

1. Understand the problems and limitations of written recipes and the importance of using judgment when you cook.
2. Discuss the structure and functions of standardized recipes.
3. Use and understand the recipes in the text to practice basic cooking techniques.
4. Measure ingredients and portions.
5. Use metric measurements.
6. Convert recipes to higher or lower yields.
7. Perform yield cost analyses.
8. Calculate raw food costs.

A. Terms

Fill in each blank with the term that is defined or described.

_____ 1. A set of instructions describing the way a particular establishment prepares a particular dish.

_____ 2. A prefix in the metric system meaning "one thousand" (1000).

_____ 3. The basic unit of weight in the metric system, equal to about 1/30 of an ounce.

_____ 4. The weight of a food item as purchased, before any trimming is done.

_____ 5. The basic unit of volume in the metric system, equal to approximately one quart.

_____ 6. A prefix in the metric system meaning "one one-thousandth" (1/1000).

_____ 7. The raw food cost or portion cost of a menu item divided by the menu price (expressed as a percent).

_____ 8. The basic unit of length in the metric system, equal to a little more than a yard.

_____ 9. The basic unit of temperature in the metric system.

_____ 10. A prefix in the metric system meaning "one tenth" (1/10).

_____ 11. The weight of a raw food item after all nonedible or all nonservable parts have been trimmed off.

_____ 12. The weight of a food item as served.

_____ 13. A prefix in the metric system meaning "one one-hundredth" (1/100).

_____ 14. The total cost of all the ingredients in a recipe, divided by the number of portions served.

B. Units of Measure

Fill in the blanks by making the correct conversions. For example:

6 tbsp = <u> 3 </u> fl. oz
18 oz = <u> 1 </u> lb <u> 2 </u> oz
32 oz = <u> 2 </u> lb <u> 0 </u> oz

1. 2¼ lb   = _____ oz

2. ½ cup   = _____ fl. oz

3. 57 oz   = _____ lb _____ oz

4. 36 fl. oz = _____ pt _____ fl. oz

5. 7¾ qt   = _____ fl. oz

6. 15 tsp   = _____ tbsp

7. 22 oz   = _____ lb _____ oz

8. 256 fl. oz = _____ gal

9. 12 qt   = _____ gal

10. 8 lb 8 oz = _____ oz

11. 3¾ lb   = _____ lb _____ oz

12. 9 cups = _____ pt

13. 44 oz   = _____ lb _____ oz

14. 16 cups = _____ qt

15. ¾ qt   = _____ fl. oz

16. 2.6 kg = _____ g

17. 3.5 L   = _____ mL

18. 6 dL   = _____ L

19. 1250 g = _____ kg

20. 22 cm = _____ mm

21. .55 kg = _____ g

22. 6500 g = _____ kg

23. 750 dL = _____ L

24. 5 cL   = _____ dL

25. 4.6 kg   = _____ g

26. 550 g   = _____ kg

27. 750 mL   = _____ L

28. 50 mm   = _____ cm

29. 1.225 kg   = _____ g

30. 0.6 L   = _____ mL

C. Recipe Conversion

The following ingredients and quantities are for gazpacho, a cold vegetable soup. The recipe yields 12 portions at 6 oz each. Convert the recipe to the yields indicated.

	12 portions, 6 oz each	30 portions, 6 oz each	36 portions, 8 oz each
Tomatoes	2½ lb	_____	_____
Cucumbers	1 lb	_____	_____
Onions	8 oz	_____	_____
Green peppers	4 oz	_____	_____
Crushed garlic	½ tsp	_____	_____
Bread crumbs, fresh	2 oz	_____	_____
Cold water or tomato juice	1 pt	_____	_____
Red wine vinegar	3 fl. oz	_____	_____
Olive oil	5 fl. oz	_____	_____
Salt	to taste	_____	_____
Pepper	to taste	_____	_____
Lemon juice	3 tbsp	_____	_____

Recipe Conversion—Metric

The following ingredients and quantities are for gazpacho, a cold vegetable soup. The recipe yields 12 portions at 200 mL each. Convert the recipe to the yields indicated.

	12 portions, 200 mL each	30 portions, 200 mL each	36 portions, 250 mL each
Tomatoes	1250 g	_____	_____
Cucumbers	500 g	_____	_____
Onions	300 g	_____	_____
Green peppers	125 g	_____	_____
Crushed garlic	2 mL	_____	_____
Bread crumbs, fresh	60 g	_____	_____
Cold water or tomato juice	600 mL	_____	_____
Red wine vinegar	100 mL	_____	_____
Olive oil	150 mL	_____	_____
Salt	to taste	_____	_____
Pepper	to taste	_____	_____
Lemon juice	50 mL	_____	_____

D. Food Cost Percentages

For each of the following six problems, use the two figures that are given to calculate the third figure, and fill in the blank.

Food cost percentage	Portion cost	Menu price
1. 25%	_____	$ 6.00
2. _____	$2.50	$10.00
3. 30%	$3.60	_____
4. _____	$5.12	$12.95
5. 35%	$6.48	_____
6. 28%	_____	$ 7.50

E. Portion Cost

Cost out the following recipe. For prices of the ingredients, use figures supplied by your instructor or the *Sample Prices* on pages 223–224.

ITEM: **STUFFED BAKED POTATOES**

Ingredient	Recipe Quantity	AP Quantity	Price	Total Amount
Baking potatoes, 8 oz each	40	_____	_____	_____
Butter	12 oz	_____	_____	_____
Milk	1 pt	_____	_____	_____
Dry bread crumbs	2 oz	_____	_____	_____
Parmesan cheese	2 oz	_____	_____	_____

Total cost	_____
Number of portions	40
Cost per portion	_____

Portion Cost—Metric

Cost out the following recipe. For prices of the ingredients, use figures supplied by your instructor or the "Sample Prices" on pages 223–224.

ITEM: **STUFFED BAKED POTATOES**

Ingredient	Recipe Quantity	AP Quantity	Price	Total Amount
Baking potatoes, 225 g each	40			
Butter	350 g			
Milk	500 mL			
Dry bread crumbs	50 g			
Parmesan cheese	50 g			

Total cost _____

Number of portions   40

Cost per portion _____

F. Raw Yield Test

Fill in the blanks in the following Yield Test form.

ITEM: **VEAL LEG TO SCALOPPINE**

AP weight: 34 lb   Price per lb: $5.50   Total cost: $187.00

Trim, Salvage, and Waste:

Item	Weight	Value/lb	Total value (lb × value/lb)
Fat	2 lb 12 oz	$ .05	_____
Bone	3 lb 12 oz	.30	_____
Ground veal	2 lb 8 oz	$5.29	_____
Stew meat	3 lb	$5.79	_____
Unusable trim	15 oz	0	_____
Cutting loss	_____	0	_____

Total weight of
trim, salvage,
and waste: _____

Total value of
trim, salvage,
and waste: _____

Total yield of
item (scaloppine):   20 lb 12 oz

Net cost of item: _____

Cost per lb: _____

Percentage of
increase: _____

Raw Yield Test—Metric

Fill in the blanks in the following Yield Test form.

ITEM: **VEAL LEG TO SCALOPPINE**

AP weight: 15 kg   Price per lb: $12.00   Total cost: $180.00

Trim, Salvage, and Waste:

Item	Weight	Value / kg	Total value (kg × value / kg)
Fat	1.25 kg	$ .10	_____
Bone	1.7 kg	.65	_____
Ground veal	1.2 kg	$11.49	_____
Stew meat	1.4 kg	$12.79	_____
Unusable trim	400 g	0	_____
Cutting loss	_____	0	_____

Total weight of
  trim, salvage,
  and waste: _____

Total value of
  trim, salvage,
  and waste: _____

Total yield of
  item (scaloppine):   5.95 kg

Net cost of item: _____

Cost per kg: _____

Percentage of
  increase: _____

CHAPTER 6

THE MENU

Chapter 6 introduces you to some of the basic concepts of menu planning. You should not expect to become expert menu planners with only the information in this chapter. But this introduction will help you think about the relationships between the various foods that you are learning to handle and to cook. In the long run, you want to be able not merely to cook different foods, but to prepare and present balanced, attractive meals.

After studying Chapter 6, you should be able to:

1. Explain how the makeup of a menu depends on the type of meal and on the institution using it.
2. Describe the differences between static and cycle menus, and between à la carte and table d'hôte menus.
3. List the various courses that may appear in modern menus.
4. Devise balanced menus that contain an adequate variety of foods and that can be efficiently and economically prepared.
5. Bring an awareness of basic nutritional principles to the construction of menus.

A. Terms

Fill in each blank with the term that is defined or described.

_____ 1. A menu on which each individual item is listed separately with its own price.

_____ 2. A food or group of foods served at one time or intended to be eaten at one time.

_____ 3. The amount of heat needed to raise the temperature of 1 kilogram of water by 1°C.

_____ 4. A food protein that contains all essential amino acids.

_____ 5. Any disease that is caused by the lack of a particular vitamin.

_____ 6. A menu that offers the same dishes every day.

_____ 7. A component of some foods that cannot be digested or used by the body but that is important for the proper functioning of the intestinal tract.

_____ 8. A menu on which one price for the entire meal is given, and customers may choose dishes for each course offered.

_____ 9. A menu on which prices are listed for complete meals rather than for each separate item; prices vary depending on the meal the customer chooses.

_____ 10. A group of nutrients that includes starches and sugars.

_____ 11. Two categories of fats: the first is liquid at room temperature, while the second is solid at room temperature.
_____

_____ 12. A menu that changes every day for a certain period, after which the daily menus are repeated in the same order.

B. Menu Review

1. List three types of establishments likely to have a cycle menu: _____,

_____, _____; and two types

likely to have a static menu: _____, _____.

2. Suppose you are planning a lunch menu for a small cafe in the heart of a business district where there are many offices and shops. What are three factors that will affect the kinds of foods you will include on the menu? Briefly explain each factor.

_____

_____

_____

_____

_____

_____

3. Three characteristics of foods—flavor, texture, and appearance—should be considered in order to build a menu with variety and balance (see page 91 in the textbook). For each of these factors, list *three pairs* of foods that you would serve together. Try not to use any of the examples in the text. (An example is given to get you started.)

Texture Balance:

Example: breaded, fried chicken breast (crisp breading) with buttered spinach (soft).

(a) _____

_____

(b) _____

_____

(c) _____

_____

Flavor Balance:

(a) _____

_____

(b) _____

_____

(c) _____

_____

Appearance (including color and shape) Balance:

(a) _____

_____

(b) _____

_____

(c) _____

_____

4. From the point of view of "truth in menu," what do the following terms mean?

(a) homemade: _____

_____

(b) fresh: _____

_____

(c) imported: _____

_____

(d) jumbo shrimp: _____

_____

5. List the following courses in the order in which they would be served in a formal dinner: roast rack of lamb with spring vegetables; jellied consommé; poached fillet of sole with white wine sauce; caviar; apple tart.

_____

_____

_____

_____

_____

6. The following menus are missing one or more dishes or courses. Based on what you have learned about menu balance, fill in the blanks with your own suggestions.

(a) Tomato soup

Roast prime ribs of beef

Baked potato

Vegetable: _____

(b) Cream of mushroom soup

Mixed green salad

Grilled lamb chops

Vegetable: _____

Starch: _____

(c) Shrimp cocktail

    Vegetable beef soup

    Main course: _____

      side dish(es) _____

      _____

(d) Appetizer: _____

    Mixed green salad

    Batter-fried shrimp

      Rice pilaf

      Vegetable: _____

(e) First course: _____

    Grilled salmon steak with dill butter

      Steamed rice

      Vegetable: _____

(f) Soup: _____

    Fried chicken

      Biscuits

      Corn

(g) Smoked salmon canapés

    Beef consommé

    Main course: _____

      Buttered asparagus

      Whipped potatoes

(h) Vegetable soup

    Roast pork loin with garlic and sage

      Vegetable: _____

      Starch: _____

(i) Luncheon special: macaroni and cheese

Any other course or side dish:

_____

(j) Luncheon special: hot roast beef sandwich,
potato chips

Any other course or side dish:

_____

C. Nutrition Review

1. One ounce is equal to 28.35 grams. Therefore, how many calories are supplied by 1 ounce of sugar?

_____

1 ounce of starch: _____

1 ounce of fat: _____

1 ounce of protein: _____

How many calories are supplied by 25 grams of sugar? _____

25 grams of starch: _____

25 grams of fat: _____

25 grams of protein: _____

2. For each of the following nutrients, list three major food sources:

protein: _____

_____

_____

fat: _____

_____

_____

carbohydrate: _____

_____

_____

Vitamin C: _____

_____

_____

Vitamin A: _____

_____

_____

3. What is the most important function of carbohydrates in the body? _____

_____

4. What is the most important function of proteins in the body? _____

_____

5. Why is it important to include the B vitamins and vitamin C in the diet every day? _____

_____

6. What is the body's major source of the mineral sodium? _____

Why do health experts caution us to cut back on sodium in the diet? _____

_____

7. Give three specific examples of how you, as a restaurant chef, could reduce the fat content of foods that you

prepare for your customers. _____

_____

_____

_____

_____

8. How can using the freshest, highest quality ingredients help you cook more healthful meals? _____

_____

_____

_____

9. Based on what you have learned about nutrition, what do you think the term "empty calories" means?

_____

_____

_____

10. List the categories of foods as described in the food pyramid. How many daily servings of each category of food is recommended?

_____

_____

_____

_____

_____

PRE-PREPARATION

Well-planned preproduction is one of the most important elements of food service. It is essential for efficient production and service. Be sure you know this material well. In addition, be sure to practice the knife-handling techniques introduced in Chapter 7.

After studying Chapter 7, you should be able to:

1. Explain the importance of carefully planned pre-preparation.
2. Describe the steps in planning for pre-preparation.
3. Explain the difference in pre-preparation requirements for set meal service and extended meal service.
4. Keep sharp edges on your knives.
5. Use a chef's knife to perform basic cutting techniques.
6. Understand basic precooking and marinating procedures.
7. Set up and use a standard breading station.
8. Handle convenience foods in pre-preparation operations.

A. Terms

Fill in each blank with the term that is defined or described.

_____ 1. Cut into small, thin strips, about ⅛ × ⅛ × 2½ in. (3 mm × 3 mm × 6½ cm).

_____ 2. Any food that has been partially or completely prepared or processed by the manufacturer.

_____ 3. Cut into very fine dice, about ⅛ in. (3 mm) square.

_____ **4.** French term for pre-preparation, meaning *put in place*.

_____ **5.** A semiliquid mixture containing flour or other starch, often used to coat items to be deep fried.

_____ **6.** To cut into very thin slices.

_____ **7.** To chop into very fine pieces.

_____ **8.** To soak a food in a seasoned liquid.

_____ **9.** To cut into thin but irregular strips, either with a knife or with a coarse grater.

_____ **10.** Cut into sticks, about ¼ × ¼ × 2½–3 in. (6 mm × 6 mm × 6–7½ cm).

_____ **11.** To chop coarsely.

_____ **12.** Service of a meal at which all the customers eat at one time.

_____ **13.** Service of a meal at which customers eat at different times.

_____ **14.** The preliminary processing of ingredients to the point at which they can be used in cooking.

_____ **15.** A pre-preparation technique in which an item is cooked partially and very briefly in boiling water or hot fat.

_____ **16.** The measurement of portions to ensure that the correct amount of an item is served.

_____ **17.** The basic method used to apply crumb coatings to foods before frying or sautéing.

B. True/False

T   F   **1.** One disadvantage of traditional large-batch cooking for set meal service is that hot foods deteriorate in quality when they are held at serving temperature.

T   F   **2.** For all recipes, final cooking must be started just before serving (when the waiter calls for the order) in order to produce the best quality foods.

T   F   **3.** When foods are cooked to order, the cooks don't need to begin work until the first orders come in.

T   F   **4.** A disadvantage of small-batch cooking is that it produces many leftovers.

T   F   **5.** When sharpening a knife on a stone, it is important to press down firmly on the blade.

T   F   **6.** The blade of the knife should be held at a 45-degree angle to the sharpening stone.

T   F   **7.** Most foods hold their quality better in the refrigerator than in the steam table.

T   F   **8.** After sharpening a knife with a steel, you should finish off the job with a few strokes on the stone to true the edge.

T   F   **9.** The tip of the chef's knife is used for cutting small items and for delicate work, because the blade is thinnest at the tip.

T   F   **10.** Whole spices, such as cloves and peppercorns, are more suitable for long marinations than for short ones.

T   F   **11.** Eggs are always used in batters for deep-frying.

C. Breading

In the space below, draw a diagram of a breading station.

STOCKS AND SAUCES

This is not only the first production chapter in the text, but it is also one of the most important. The techniques used in the making of stocks and sauces are the foundation of much of the work that is done in the commercial kitchen. Please study and review this material well.

After studying Chapter 8, you should be able to:

1. Prepare basic mirepoix.
2. Use a sachet or spice bag for flavoring liquids.
3. Prepare white veal or beef stock, chicken stock, fish stock, and brown stock.
4. Cool and store stocks correctly.
5. Prepare meat, chicken, and fish glazes.
6. Evaluate and use convenience bases.
7. Explain the functions of sauces.
8. Prepare white, blond, and brown roux and use them to thicken liquids.
9. Prepare and use beurre manié.
10. Thicken liquids with cornstarch and other starches.
11. Prepare and use egg yolk and cream liaison.
12. Finish a sauce with raw butter (monter au beurre).
13. Prepare the five leading sauces: Béchamel, Velouté, Brown Sauce or Espagnole, Tomato, and Hollandaise.
14. Prepare small sauces from leading sauces.
15. Prepare simple and compound butters.
16. Prepare miscellaneous hot and cold sauces and pan gravies.

A. Terms

Fill in each blank with the term that is defined or described.

_____ 1. A clear, thin liquid flavored by soluble substances extracted from meat, poultry, fish, and their bones, and from vegetables and seasonings.

_____ 2. A cheesecloth bag containing spices and herbs, used to flavor liquids.

_____ 3. A flavorful liquid, usually thickened, used to season, flavor, and enhance other foods.

_____ 4. A stock that is reduced until it coats the back of a spoon.

_____ 5. The process of boiling or simmering a liquid to evaporate part of the water.

_____ 6. The uniform mixture of two unmixable substances, usually two liquids.

_____ 7. A mixture of raw butter and various flavoring ingredients.

_____ 8. A basic sauce used in the production of other sauces.

_____ 9. A finished sauce, consisting of one of the basic sauces plus flavorings and other finishing ingredients.

_____ 10. A basic sauce consisting of thickened white stock.

_____ 11. A basic sauce consisting primarily of cooked, thickened milk.

_____ 12. A mixture of rough-cut or diced vegetables (usually including onion, celery, and carrot), and sometimes herbs and spices; this mixture is used for flavoring.

_____ 13. A combination of fresh herbs, tied together, used for flavoring.

_____ 14. A substance, extracted from connective tissue during stock making, which gives body to stock and which causes good stock to thicken or solidify when chilled.

_____ 15. The process of raising a stock pot onto blocks in a cold-water bath, so that the cold water can circulate better and cool the stock more quickly.

_____ 16. Unthickened juices from a roast, seasoned and served with the roast.

_____ 17. Term used on menus to describe meats served with the juices described in number 16.

_____ 18. A cooked mixture of equal parts flour and butter, used to thicken liquids.

_____ 19. An uncooked mixture of equal parts flour and raw butter, used to thicken liquids.

_____ 20. Brown stock that has been reduced until it is thick enough to coat the back of a spoon.

_____ **21.** Chicken stock that has been reduced until it is thick enough to coat the back of a spoon.

_____ **22.** A mixture of cold water and starch, such as cornstarch, used to thicken a liquid.

_____ **23.** A mixture of cream and egg yolks, used to thicken and enrich a sauce or soup.

_____ **24.** A type of starch, used to thicken liquids, that keeps its binding or thickening power even after having been frozen.

_____ **25.** A term meaning *until dry*, used in connection with the term defined in number 5.

_____ **26.** A mixture of half brown sauce and half brown stock, reduced by half.

_____ **27.** To swirl a liquid in a pan to dissolve cooked particles of food remaining on the bottom.

_____ **28.** To finish a sauce by swirling in a little raw butter until it melts and blends in.

_____ **29.** A sauce made by thickening brown stock with cornstarch or similar starch.

_____ **30.** A sauce made with the juices or drippings of the meat or poultry with which it is served.

_____ **31.** Butter that is heated until it turns light brown.

_____ **32.** Purified butterfat, made by melting raw butter and removing the water and milk solids.

_____ **33.** A sauce made by whipping a large amount of butter into a small amount of a flavorful reduction.

B. Stock-Making Review

Stock making is one of the most fundamental of all kitchen techniques, and you should be able, without hesitation, to describe in detail how to make it.

List the ingredients and the proper quantities to make 1 gal (or 4 L), first of white stock, then of brown stock. For each product, use the space after the ingredients to list the steps in production. It is not necessary to explain the steps, as the textbook does, but be sure to include all the steps, and number the steps to make the procedure easier to read.

White Stock

Ingredients: Quantities to make 1 gal (4 L)

Procedure:

Brown Stock

Ingredients: Quantities to make 1 gal (4 L)

Procedure:

C. Sauce Families I

To review the composition of the five Leading Sauces, fill in the names of the sauces, the liquid that forms the base of the sauce, and the thickening agent.

Leading Sauce	Liquid	Thickening Agent
_____	_____	_____
_____	_____	_____
_____	_____	_____
_____	_____	_____
_____	_____	_____

D. Sauce Families II

Review the composition of Small Sauces by completing the following chart. In the left column are listed a number of Small Sauces. For each one, list the Leading Sauce that it is based on, as well as the most important flavoring or finishing ingredient(s).

Small Sauce	Leading Sauce	Principal Flavoring
1. Mornay	_____	_____
2. Robert	_____	_____
3. Chasseur	_____	_____
4. Suprême	_____	_____
5. Madeira	_____	_____
6. Bercy (white)	_____	_____
7. Aurora	_____	_____
8. Bordelaise	_____	_____
9. Nantua	_____	_____
10. Mousseline	_____	_____
11. Foyot	_____	_____

12. Creole _____ _____

13. White Wine _____ _____

14. Allemande _____ _____

15. Cream _____ _____

16. Lyonnaise _____ _____

17. Mushroom (brown) _____ _____

18. Maltaise _____ _____

19. Hungarian _____ _____

20. Portugaise _____ _____

21. Diable _____ _____

22. Mustard _____ _____

23. Choron _____ _____

24. Bercy (brown) _____ _____

E. Hollandaise Review

In the following space, explain how to make Hollandaise Sauce. Be sure to include all necessary steps, and number the steps to make the procedure easier to read. Include ingredient quantities if your instructor asks you to do so.

F. Recipe Conversion

The following ingredients and quantities are for a barbecue sauce recipe that yields ½ gal. Convert the recipe to the yields indicated.

	½ gal	1½ gal	1 quart
Tomato purée	1 qt	_____	_____
Water	1 pt	_____	_____
Worcestershire sauce	⅔ cup	_____	_____
Cider vinegar	½ cup	_____	_____
Vegetable oil	½ cup	_____	_____
Onion	8 oz	_____	_____
Garlic, crushed	4 tsp	_____	_____
Sugar	2 oz	_____	_____
Dry mustard	1 tbsp	_____	_____
Chili powder	2 tsp	_____	_____
Black pepper	1 tsp	_____	_____
Salt	to taste	_____	_____

Recipe Conversion—Metric

The following ingredients and quantities are for a barbecue sauce recipe that yields 2 L. Convert the recipe to the yields indicated.

	2 liters	6 liters	1 liter
Tomato purée	1 L	_____	_____
Water	500 mL	_____	_____
Worcestershire sauce	175 mL	_____	_____
Cider vinegar	125 mL	_____	_____
Vegetable oil	125 mL	_____	_____
Onion	250 g	_____	_____
Garlic, crushed	20 mL	_____	_____
Sugar	60 g	_____	_____
Dry mustard	15 mL	_____	_____
Chili powder	10 mL	_____	_____
Black pepper	5 mL	_____	_____
Salt	to taste	_____	_____

G. Portion Cost

Cost out the following recipe. For prices of the ingredients, use figures supplied by your instructor or the *Sample Prices* on pages 223–224. For the sake of this exercise, assume that the quantities given for the vegetables are AP quantities (see pages 80 and 84 in the textbook).

ITEM: **SWEET AND SOUR SAUCE**

Yield: 1 qt

Ingredient	Recipe Quantity	AP Quantity	Price	Total Amount
Chicken stock	1 qt	_____	_____	_____
Cornstarch	1 oz	_____	_____	_____
Sugar	8 oz	_____	_____	_____
Soy sauce	2 oz	_____	_____	_____
Green bell pepper	2 oz	_____	_____	_____
Red bell pepper	2 oz	_____	_____	_____
Onion	4 oz	_____	_____	_____
Red wine vinegar	½ cup	_____	_____	_____
Ginger	½ tsp (¹⁄₂₅ oz)	_____	_____	_____
Salt	to taste	_____	_____	_____
Pepper	to taste	_____	_____	_____

Total cost _____

Number of 2-oz portions _____

Cost per portion _____

Portion Cost—Metric

Cost out the following recipe. For prices of the ingredients, use figures supplied by your instructor or the *Sample Prices* on pages 223–224. For the sake of this exercise, assume that the quantities given for the vegetables are AP quantities (see pages 80 and 84 in the textbook).

ITEM: **SWEET AND SOUR SAUCE**

Yield: 1 L

Ingredient	Recipe Quantity	AP Quantity	Price	Total Amount
Chicken stock	1 L	_____	_____	_____
Cornstarch	25 g	_____	_____	_____
Sugar	250 g	_____	_____	_____
Soy sauce	75 mL	_____	_____	_____
Green bell pepper	60 g	_____	_____	_____
Red bell pepper	60 g	_____	_____	_____
Onion	125 g	_____	_____	_____
Red wine vinegar	125 mL	_____	_____	_____
Ginger	2 mL (1 g)	_____	_____	_____
Salt	to taste	_____	_____	_____
Pepper	to taste	_____	_____	_____

Total cost _____

Number of
50-mL portions _____

Cost per portion _____

SOUPS

The procedures for some kinds of soup are fairly easy to learn, so these are some of the first products that culinary students learn. On the other hand, some other soup-making procedures are much more difficult, and require more study and practice. But whether you are learning simple procedures or complicated ones, you must pay close attention to the proper techniques in order to make quality soups.

After studying Chapter 9, you should be able to:

1. Describe the major categories of soups.
2. Serve soups properly.
3. Prepare clarified consommé.
4. Prepare vegetable soups and other clear soups.
5. Prepare cream soups.
6. Prepare purée soups.
7. Prepare bisques, chowders, specialty soups, and national soups.

A. Terms

Fill in each blank with the term that is defined or described.

_____ **1.** A thickened cream soup made from shellfish.

_____ **2.** A rich, flavorful stock or broth that has been clarified to make it clear and transparent.

_____ **3.** The mixture of ingredients used to clarify a stock to make the product described in number 2.

_____ **4.** The mixture described in number 3, after it has coagulated and floated to the surface of the stock.

_____ **5.** A soup that is thickened by puréeing one or more of its ingredients.

_____ **6.** A clear, seasoned stock or broth with the addition of one or more vegetables and sometimes meat or poultry products or starches.

_____ **7.** A general French term for soup, often used to refer to a thick, hearty soup.

_____ **8.** A soup that is thickened with roux or other thickening agent and contains milk and/or cream.

_____ **9.** A cold soup made of puréed leeks and onions with cream.

_____ **10.** A clarified soup, as described in number 2, flavored strongly with tomato.

_____ **11.** A type of hearty American soup often containing seafood, potatoes, and milk.

_____ **12.** Another name for Purée of Carrot Soup.

_____ **13.** A specialty soup, from Russia, containing beets as a major ingredient.

B. Consommé Review

The procedure for clarifying consommé is one that you should know well. Using numbered steps, explain how to make consommé. Be sure to include all the necessary steps. Include ingredient quantities if your instructor asks you to do so.

C. True/False

T   F   **1.** Most vegetable soups should be cooked a long time so that the broth will develop flavor.

T   F   **2.** The four basic ingredients used to clarify a stock are ground meat, mirepoix, tomato product, and an acid ingredient.

T   F   **3.** When you are making chicken noodle soup, it is best to cook the noodles separately if you want to keep the broth clear.

T   F   **4.** Beef loin is the best meat to use for clarifying stock.

T   F   **5.** A typical appetizer-size portion of soup is 6 to 8 oz (175 to 250 mL).

T   F   **6.** The best way to maintain the quality of a large quantity of vegetable soup is to keep it hot in a steam table throughout the service period.

T   F   **7.** Protein coagulation is the process that makes possible the clarification of stock.

T   F   **8.** A well-made consommé has a rich, dark brown color.

T   F   **9.** Based on the production method, lobster bisque could be classified as a cream soup.

T   F   **10.** When it is being clarified, a consommé should be brought to a rapid boil so that the proteins will coagulate properly.

T   F   **11.** Consommé Printanière is garnished with various spring vegetables.

T   F   **12.** For best flavor, it is always best to include as many different vegetables as possible in a clear vegetable soup.

T   F   **13.** Starch thickeners help to stabilize milk and cream so that they are less likely to curdle.

T   F   **14.** Mirepoix for cream soups should be browned lightly to develop flavor.

T   F   **15.** A starchy product is usually one of the ingredients in a purée soup.

D. Cream Soup Review

Explain how to make Cream of Carrot Soup. Use either Method 1 or Method 2, or whichever method your instructor assigns. Write the procedure in the form of numbered steps. If your instructor asks you to do so, include ingredient quantities.

E. Recipe Conversion

The following ingredients and quantities are for a Potato Chowder recipe that yields 24 portions, 8 oz each. Convert the recipe to the yields indicated.

	24 portions, 8 oz each	36 portions, 8 oz each	24 portions, 6 oz each
Salt pork	8 oz	_____	_____
Onions	12 oz	_____	_____
Celery	3 oz	_____	_____
Flour	4 oz	_____	_____
Chicken stock	3½ qt	_____	_____
Potatoes	3 lb	_____	_____
Milk	3 pt	_____	_____
Heavy cream	1 cup	_____	_____
Chopped parsley	4 tbsp	_____	_____

Recipe Conversion—Metric

The following ingredients and quantities are for a Potato Chowder recipe that yields 24 portions, 250 mL each. Convert the recipe to the yields indicated.

	24 portions, 250 mL each	36 portions, 250 mL each	24 portions, 175 mL each
Salt pork	250 g	_____	_____
Onions	375 g	_____	_____
Celery	100 g	_____	_____
Flour	124 g	_____	_____
Chicken stock	3.5 L	_____	_____
Potatoes	1.5 kg	_____	_____
Milk	1.5 L	_____	_____
Heavy cream	250 mL	_____	_____
Chopped parsley	60 mL	_____	_____

F. Portion Cost

Cost out the following recipe. For prices of the ingredients, use figures supplied by your instructor or the *Sample Prices* on pages 223–224.

ITEM: **BORSCHT**

Ingredient	Recipe Quantity	AP Quantity	Price	Total Amount
Beef brisket	2 lb	_____	_____	_____
Beef stock	3½ qt	_____	_____	_____
Butter	4 oz	_____	_____	_____
Onion, EP*	8 oz	_____	_____	_____
Leeks, EP*	8 oz	_____	_____	_____
Cabbage, EP*	8 oz	_____	_____	_____
Beets	2 No. 2½ cans	_____	_____	_____
Tomato purée	4 oz	_____	_____	_____
Red wine vinegar	4 oz	_____	_____	_____
Sugar	1 oz	_____	_____	_____
Sour cream	12 oz	_____	_____	_____

Total cost _____

Number of portions 24

Cost per portion _____

Note: Remember that you need AP weights of all ingredients (see pages 80 and 84 in the textbook). Let's assume that you kept a record of the quantities needed when you made this recipe:
To get 8 oz EP onions, you needed 9 oz AP.
To get 8 oz EP leeks, you needed 1 lb AP.
To get 8 oz EP cabbage, you needed 10 oz AP.

Portion Cost—Metric

Cost out the following recipe. For prices of the ingredients, either use figures supplied by your instructor, or use the *Sample Prices* on pages 223–224.

ITEM: **BORSCHT**

Ingredient	Recipe Quantity	AP Quantity	Price	Total Amount
Beef brisket	1 kg			
Beef stock	3.5 L			
Butter	100 g			
Onion, EP*	250 g			
Leeks, EP*	250 g			
Cabbage, EP*	250 g			
Beets	2 No. 2½ cans			
Tomato purée	125 g			
Red wine vinegar	125 mL			
Sugar	25 g			
Sour cream	400 g			

Total cost _____

Number of portions   24

Cost per portion _____

Note: Remember that you need AP weights of all ingredients (see pages 80 and 84 in the textbook). Let's assume that you kept a record of the quantities needed when you made this recipe:

To get 250 g EP onions, you needed 275 g AP.
To get 250 g EP leeks, you needed 500 g AP.
To get 250 g EP cabbage, you needed 300 g AP.

UNDERSTANDING MEATS

Meats are such a large area of study that we have divided the subject matter into two chapters. This first chapter concentrates on basic product information. In particular, it discusses the general characteristics of the four most important meats—beef, lamb, veal, and pork. The great variety of meat cuts may be somewhat confusing at first, so careful review is called for.

After studying Chapter 10, you should be able to:

1. Describe the composition and structure of meat and tell how it relates to meat selection and cooking methods.

2. Use the federal meat inspection and grading system to help you select and purchase meats.

3. Explain the significance of aging meats.

4. Identify the primal cuts of beef, lamb, veal, and pork, and list the major fabricated cuts obtained from each of them.

5. Select appropriate cooking methods for the most important meat cuts, based on the meat's tenderness and other characteristics.

6. Determine doneness in cooked meats.

7. Store meats for maximum shelf life.

A. Terms

Fill in each blank with the term that is defined or described.

_____ 1. In a piece of meat, the fat that is deposited within the muscle tissue.

_____ 2. A type of connective tissue in meats that dissolves when cooked with moisture.

_____ 3. A type of connective tissue that does not break down or dissolve when cooked.

_____ 4. A government procedure that checks the wholesomeness of meat, to make sure that it is fit to eat.

_____ 5. A government procedure that checks the quality of meat.

_____ 6. Meat that has not had enough time after slaughter to develop tenderness and flavor.

_____ 7. One of the primary divisions of meat quarters, foresaddles, hindsaddles, and carcasses as they are broken down into smaller cuts.

_____ 8. The continued rise of a roast's internal temperature after it has been removed from the oven.

_____ 9. The name given to the degree of doneness of a piece of meat that is cooked on the outside but still uncooked or barely cooked on the inside.

_____ 10. A disease that could be transmitted by eating undercooked pork.

_____ 11. The four-word term that the letters IMPS stand for.

_____

_____

_____

_____ 12. A grading system that indicates how much usable meat a carcass has in proportion to fat.

_____ 13. The process of inserting strips of fat into a piece of meat, usually a cut of meat that has little of its own fat.

_____ 14. The process of tying sheets of fat over the surface of a cut of meat that does not have its own natural fat cover.

B. Short-Answer Questions

Fill in the blanks to complete the following statements. You may need more than one word per blank.

1. The most accurate way to test the doneness of a roast is to _____ .

2. As meat is aged, it gradually becomes tenderer. This is caused by _____ , which are naturally present in the meat.

3. _____ is not aged because it doesn't have enough fat cover to protect it from drying out.

4. A meat is naturally tender if it comes from a _____ animal or if it comes from a muscle that had _____ exercise.

5. Quality grading of meats _____ (is / is not) required by law.

6. Some connective tissues can be broken down by heat, by acids, or by _____ .

7. The top grade of beef is _____ . The next two grades, in order, are _____ and _____ .

8. The top three grades of veal, starting with the best, are _____ , _____ , and _____ .

9. The top three grades of lamb, starting with the best, are _____ , _____ , and _____ .

10. The first cut made to break down a carcass of veal is located between _____ _____ . This divides the carcass into two pieces called the _____ and the _____ .

11. The first cut made to break down a carcass of beef is to divide it into two halves, called _____ , by cutting it _____ .

12. The major bones in a primal rib of beef are _____ _____ .

13. The bone that forms the stem of the T in a T-bone steak is called the _____ .

14. The major bones in a full loin of beef are _____

_____ .

15. The full loin of beef may be divided into two parts, called the _____ and the _____ .

16. The standard full rack of lamb contains how many ribs? _____

17. The major bones in a primal leg of veal are _____

_____ .

18. Two examples of beef cuts that are almost always cooked by moist-heat methods are _____

and _____ .

19. Two examples of beef cuts that are almost always cooked by dry-heat methods are _____

and _____ .

20. The usual method used to test the doneness of a steak being cooked on a grill is _____ .

C. Beef Primal Cuts

Cuts are identified by numbers in the following beef chart. In each of the numbered blanks after the chart, write the name of the cut corresponding to the number in the chart.

1. _____   5. _____   9. _____

2. _____   6. _____   10. _____

3. _____   7. _____

4. _____   8. _____

D. Pork Cuts

Cuts are identified by numbers in the following pork chart. In each of the numbered blanks after the chart, write the name of the cut corresponding to the number in the chart.

1. _____   6. _____

2. _____   7. _____

3. _____   8. _____

4. _____   9. _____

5. _____   10. _____

E. The Round or Leg

Identify the various parts in the following diagram of a round steak, and fill in the numbered blanks with the names of the parts.

1. _____

2. _____

3. _____

4. _____

5. _____

F. Fabricated Cuts

In the blank following the name of each cut, write the name of the primal cut from which it is taken.

1. Beef shoulder clod   _____

2. Lamb rib chop   _____

3. Beef sirloin steak   _____

4. Veal loin chop   _____

5. Beef rump   _____

6. Canadian-style bacon   _____

7. Boneless lamb rolled shoulder roast   _____

8. Corned beef brisket   _____

9. Beef porterhouse steak   _____

10. Beef flank steak   _____

11. Pork rib chop   _____

12. Beef knuckle   _____

13. Beef hamburger   _____

14. Smoked daisy ham   _____

15. Bacon   _____

16. Leg of lamb roast   _____

17. Veal scaloppine   _____

18. Beef tenderloin steak   _____

19. Beef short ribs   _____

20. Beef top round   _____

21. Smoked picnic ham   _____

22. Veal saddle roast   _____

23. Beef T-bone steak   _____

24. Beef strip loin steak   _____

25. Lamb sirloin chop   _____

G. Raw Yield Test

Fill in the blanks in the following Yield Test form. (Instructions for completing this form are in Chapter 5 of the textbook, pages 80–82.)

ITEM: **BEEF STRIP LOIN (BONE IN) REGULAR TO TRIMMED STRIP LOIN STEAKS**

AP weight: 18 lb   Price per lb: $2.99   Total cost: $53.82

Trim, Salvage, and Waste:

Item	Weight	Value/lb	Total value (lb × value/lb)
Fat	2 lb 9 oz	$ .07	_____
Bone	4 lb 2 oz	.24	_____
Ground beef	11 oz	$2.39	_____
Cutting loss	_____	0	_____

Total weight of trim, salvage, and waste: _____   Total value of trim, salvage, and waste: _____

Total yield of item (steaks):   10 lb 8 oz

Net cost of item: _____

Cost per lb: _____

Percentage of increase: _____

Raw Yield Test—Metric

Fill in the blanks in the following Yield Test form. (Instructions for completing this form are in Chapter 5 of the textbook, pages 80–82, and in Appendix 4, page 799.)

ITEM: BEEF STRIP LOIN (BONE IN) REGULAR TO TRIMMED STRIP LOIN STEAKS

AP weight: 8 kg   Price per kg: $6.79   Total cost: $54.32

Trim, Salvage, and Waste:

Item	Weight	Value / kg	Total value (kg × value / kg)
Fat	1.2 kg	$ .15	_____
Bone	1.9 kg	.55	_____
Ground beef	350 g	$5.25	_____
Cutting loss	_____	0	_____

Total weight of trim,
   salvage, and waste: _____

Total value of trim,
   salvage, and waste: _____

Total yield of item (steaks):   4.5 kg

Net cost of item: _____

Cost per kg: _____

Percentage of increase: _____

Recipe Conversion—Metric

The following ingredients and quantities are for a Roast Stuffed Lamb Shoulder recipe that yields 10 portions, 150 g each. Convert the recipe to the yields indicated.

	10 portions, 150 g each	30 portions, 150 g each	75 portions, 125 g each
Onion	125 g		
Garlic	5 mL		
Oil	50 mL		
Bread crumbs, fresh	100 g		
Chopped parsley	75 mL		
Rosemary	2 mL		
Black pepper	1 mL		
Salt	2 mL		
Eggs, beaten	1		
Boneless lamb shoulder	2 kg		
Mirepoix	250 g		
Flour	50 g		
Brown stock	1 L		
Tomatoes, canned	125 g		

F. Portion Cost

Cost out the following recipe. For prices of the ingredients, use figures supplied by your instructor or the *Sample Prices* on pages 223–224.

ITEM: **CHILE CON CARNE**

Ingredient	Recipe Quantity	AP Quantity	Price	Total Amount
Onion, EP*	2½ lb	_____	_____	_____
Green pepper, EP*	1¼ lb	_____	_____	_____
Vegetable oil	4 oz	_____	_____	_____
Ground beef	5 lb	_____	_____	_____
Tomatoes	#10 can	_____	_____	_____
Tomato paste	10 oz	_____	_____	_____
Beef stock	2½ pt	_____	_____	_____
Chili powder	3 oz	_____	_____	_____

Total cost	_____
Number of portions	24
Cost per portion	_____

Note: Remember that you need AP weights of all ingredients (see pages 80 and 84 in the text). Let's assume that you kept a record of the quantities needed when you made this recipe:

To get 2½ lb EP onions, you needed 2 lb 12 oz AP.
To get 1¼ lb EP green pepper, you needed 1½ lb AP.

Portion Cost—Metric

Cost out the following recipe. For prices of the ingredients, use figures supplied by your instructor or the *Sample Prices* on pages 223–224.

ITEM: CHILE CON CARNE

Ingredient	Recipe Quantity	AP Quantity	Price	Total Amount
Onion, EP*	1.25 kg	_____	_____	_____
Green pepper, EP*	600 g	_____	_____	_____
Vegetable oil	125 mL	_____	_____	_____
Ground beef	2.5 kg	_____	_____	_____
Tomatoes	#10 can	_____	_____	_____
Tomato paste	300 g	_____	_____	_____
Beef stock	1.25 L	_____	_____	_____
Chili powder	100 g	_____	_____	_____
			Total cost	_____
			Number of portions	24
			Cost per portion	_____

Note: Remember that you need AP weights of all ingredients (see pages 80 and 84 in the text). Let's assume that you kept a record of the quantities needed when you made this recipe:

To get 1.25 kg EP onions, you needed 1.5 kg AP.
To get 600 g EP green pepper, you needed 700 g AP.

UNDERSTANDING POULTRY

The subject of poultry is divided into two chapters, just as the subject of meats is. Unlike the first meat chapter, however, this first poultry chapter is quite short. One of the reasons for this is that there is not such a great variety of different cuts of poultry to learn as there is for meats. Furthermore, much of this chapter is taken up with trussing and cutting techniques, which need hands-on practice rather than written study questions.

After studying Chapter 12, you should be able to:

1. Explain the differences between "light meat" and "dark meat," and describe how these differences affect cooking.

2. Use four techniques that help keep chicken or turkey breast moist while roasting.

3. Identify any domestic poultry item with reference to its kind, class, and style.

4. Store poultry items properly.

5. Determine doneness in cooked poultry.

6. Truss poultry for cooking.

7. Cut up chicken into parts.

A. Terms

Fill in each blank with the term that is defined or described.

_____ 1. A government procedure that checks the wholesomeness of poultry, to make sure that it is fit to eat.

_____ 2. A government procedure that checks the quality of poultry.

_____   **3.** The market term indicating the amount of cleaning and processing a poultry item has had.

_____   **4.** The market term indicating the species (such as chicken, turkey, or duck) of a poultry item.

_____   **5.** The market term that indicates the relative age and sometimes the sex of a poultry item.

_____   **6.** A castrated male chicken.

_____   **7.** A mature female chicken.

_____   **8.** A mature male chicken.

_____   **9.** A young pigeon.

_____   **10.** A type of domestic poultry related to the pheasant.

_____   **11.** The process of tying the legs and wings of a poultry item against the body to make a compact shape for cooking.

_____   **12.** A common name for the nugget of tender meat in the hollow of the hip bone.

_____   **13.** A special breed of young chicken, often marketed at about 1 lb in weight.

B. Short-Answer Questions

1. A mature chicken of about 10 months of age is almost always cooked by what kind of cooking method? _____

2. Which of the major parts of a chicken has the most connective tissue? _____

3. The highest U.S.D.A. grade of chicken is _____ .

4. What is the best way to thaw a frozen capon that is vacuum packed in plastic? _____

_____

5. What is the weight range for young turkey? _____

6. What class of duck is best for roasting, and what does one of these ducks weigh? _____

7. At what temperature should frozen turkey be stored? _____

8. A large roasted bird is done when a meat thermometer inserted into _____

registers the temperature of _____ .

9. Which disease-causing bacteria is most often associated with poultry? _____ What precaution

should be taken to avoid spreading this disease? _____

_____

10. What is the best way to hold fresh chickens in storage?

_____

COOKING POULTRY

In this chapter, our examination shifts from product information to cooking techniques. The basic cooking methods, first discussed in Chapter 4, are applied to a range of poultry items.

After studying Chapter 13, you should be able to:

1. Cook poultry by roasting and baking.
2. Cook poultry by broiling and grilling.
3. Cook poultry by sautéing, pan-frying, and deep-frying.
4. Cook poultry by simmering and poaching.
5. Cook poultry by braising.
6. Prepare dressings and stuffings.

A. Terms

Fill in each blank with the term that is defined or described.

_____ 1. The common menu name for duckling that is roasted and served with an orange-flavored brown sauce.

_____ 2. The menu name for a spicy broiled chicken dish that is coated with mustard and bread crumbs and usually served with a spicy brown sauce.

_____ 3. A chicken stew that is served with a pastry cover.

_____ 4. A white chicken stew cooked by the braising method, but without browning the chicken, and served in a white sauce.

_____ **5.** A chicken stew prepared by the simmering method and served in a white sauce.

_____ **6.** A chicken stew as described in number 5, garnished with asparagus tips.

_____ **7.** A mature female chicken, which must be cooked by a moist-heat method to be made tender.

_____ **8.** The menu name for a chicken stew in a white sauce garnished with pimientos.

_____ **9.** Chicken braised in red wine, garnished with small onions, mushrooms, and bacon.

_____ **10.** A dish consisting of chopped, cooked turkey bound in a stiff white sauce, shaped, breaded, and deep-fried.

_____ **11.** Chicken served with a brown sauce flavored with white wine, shallots, mushrooms, and tomatoes.

_____ **12.** The side of a piece of food that is to be face up on a plate when served.

B. Short-Answer Questions

1. What size chicken is best for deep-frying? _____

_____

2. When you are sautéing a boneless breast of chicken, which side of the chicken breast should be browned first,

for best appearance? _____

3. At what oven temperature should a 5-lb (2.3-kg) chicken be roasted? _____

4. A basic bread dressing or stuffing is made of _____ , _____ ,

_____ , and _____ , plus herbs, seasonings, and sometimes eggs.

5. If a chicken is stuffed before roasting, it is necessary to _____ the roasting time.

6. Baked, refrigerated poultry dressing that is to be heated for service must be reheated to an internal temper-

ature of _____ . The reason for this is _____ .

_____

7. _____ is a cooking method similar to simmering but requiring less liquid and a lower temperature.

8. Chicken Cacciatora is cooked by the _____ method.

9. In a classic chicken fricassée, the sauce is enriched by adding a _____ , and it is seasoned with salt, white pepper, a little nutmeg, and lemon juice.

10. It could be dangerous to use sheet pans for roasting ducks, because _____

_____ .

11. If grilled chicken becomes well browned on the outside before it is completely cooked on the inside, it may

be finished by removing it from the grill and _____

_____ .

12. The deep-fryer should be set at a temperature of _____ for deep-frying chicken.

13. Very small poultry items are generally roasted at a _____ temperature.

C. Recipe Conversion

The following ingredients and quantities are for a Chicken à la King recipe that yields 25 portions at 8 oz each. Convert the recipe to the yields indicated.

	25 portions, 8 oz each	10 portions, 8 oz each	15 portions, 10 oz each
Butter, clarified	10 oz		
Onion	3 oz		
Green pepper	10 oz		
Flour	8 oz		
Chicken stock	2½ qt		
Milk	2½ cups		
Mushrooms	1 lb		
Butter	4 oz		
Light cream	2½ cups		
Pimientos, drained	4 oz		
Cooked chicken meat	5 lb		
Sherry wine	4 oz		
Salt	to taste		
Pepper	to taste		

Recipe Conversion—Metric

The following ingredients and quantities are for a Chicken à la King recipe that yields 25 portions at 250 g each. Convert the recipe to the yields indicated.

	25 portions, 250 g each	10 portions, 250 g each	15 portions, 300 g each
Butter, clarified	300 g		
Onion	100 g		
Green pepper	300 g		
Flour	250 g		
Chicken stock	2.5 L		
Milk	650 mL		
Mushrooms	500 g		
Butter	125 g		
Light cream	600 mL		
Pimientos, drained	124 g		
Cooked chicken meat	2.5 kg		
Sherry wine	125 mL		
Salt	to taste		
Pepper	to taste		

D. Portion Cost

In order to cost out the following recipe, we need to know the cost of cooked chicken meat. But let's assume we purchased and cooked fresh fowls in order to make the recipe. In order to cost the recipe, we first must do a cooked yield test, as discussed in Chapter 5 of the textbook, pages 83–84.

In the following shortened version of the cooked yield test form, use the figures given to calculate the cost per pound of the cooked chicken. Then use this figure to cost the recipe.

ITEM: **SIMMERED FRESH FOWL**

Net raw weight: 5 lb 4 oz   Cost per lb (raw): $ .89

Total net cost: $4.67

Weight as served (cooked meat): 1 lb 12 oz

Cooked cost per pound: _____

Cost out the following recipe. For prices of the ingredients, use figures supplied by your instructor or the *Sample Prices* on pages 223–224.

ITEM: **CHICKEN TETRAZZINI**

Ingredient	Recipe Quantity	AP Quantity	Price	Total Amount
Cooked chicken	5 lb	_____	_____	_____
Chicken stock	2½ qt	_____	_____	_____
Flour	4 oz	_____	_____	_____
Butter	10 oz	_____	_____	_____
Mushrooms	2 lb	_____	_____	_____
Egg yolks*	3	_____	_____	_____
Heavy cream	2½ cups	_____	_____	_____
Sherry	2 oz	_____	_____	_____
Spaghetti	2½ lb	_____	_____	_____
Parmesan cheese	8 oz	_____	_____	_____

Total cost	_____
Number of portions	40
Cost per portion	_____

Note: For the sake of this exercise, use the cost of whole eggs as the cost of the yolks. If you then use the egg whites in another recipe, you would enter a cost of zero for the whites when costing that recipe. This is because you are accounting for the cost of the whole eggs in the chicken recipe.

Portion Cost—Metric

In order to cost out the following recipe, we need to know the cost of cooked chicken meat. But let's assume we purchased and cooked fresh fowls in order to make the recipe. In order to cost the recipe, we first must do a cooked yield test, as discussed in Chapter 5 of the textbook, pages 83–84.

In the following shortened version of the cooked yield test form, use the figures given to calculate the cost per pound of the cooked chicken. Then use this figure to cost the recipe.

ITEM: **SIMMERED FRESH FOWL**

Net raw weight: 2.4 kg   Cost per kg (raw): $1.95

Total net cost: $4.68

Weight as served (cooked meat): 800 g

Cooked cost per kilogram: _____

Cost out the following recipe. For prices of the ingredients, use figures supplied by your instructor or the *Sample Prices* on pages 223–224.

ITEM: **CHICKEN TETRAZZINI**

Ingredient	Recipe Quantity	AP Quantity	Price	Total Amount
Cooked chicken	2.5 kg	_____	_____	_____
Chicken stock	2.5 L	_____	_____	_____
Flour	125 g	_____	_____	_____
Butter	300 g	_____	_____	_____
Mushrooms	1 kg	_____	_____	_____
Egg yolks*	3	_____	_____	_____
Heavy cream	600 mL	_____	_____	_____
Sherry	50 mL	_____	_____	_____
Spaghetti	1.25 kg	_____	_____	_____
Parmesan cheese	250 g	_____	_____	_____

Total cost	_____
Number of portions	40
Cost per portion	_____

Note: For the sake of this exercise, use the cost of whole eggs as the cost of the yolks. If you then use the egg whites in another recipe, you would enter a cost of zero for the whites when costing that recipe. This is because you are accounting for the cost of the whole eggs in the chicken recipe.

CHAPTER 14

UNDERSTANDING FISH AND SHELLFISH

The composition and structure of fish and seafood products is quite different from that of meat and poultry. Furthermore, fish products are much more perishable than meat is. Consequently, this subject requires special study, so that when you apply the basic cooking techniques to seafood products, you will be able to adjust them to fit these unique products.

After studying Chapter 14, you should be able to:

1. Explain how the cooking qualities of fish are affected by its lack of connective tissue.
2. Determine doneness in cooked fish.
3. Select appropriate cooking methods for fat and lean fish.
4. Recognize the basic market forms of fish.
5. Dress and fillet round fish and flat fish.
6. Recognize the most common varieties of fin fish in American food service.
7. Check fish for freshness.
8. Store fish and fish products properly.
9. Understand the popular varieties of shellfish, including their characteristics, handling, and special cooking procedures.
10. Open oysters and clams, split lobster, and peel and devein shrimp.

A. Terms

Fill in each blank with the term that is defined or described.

_____ 1. The family of sea animals that includes soft animals that live inside a pair of hinged shells.

_____ 2. The family of sea animals that have segmented shells and jointed legs.

_____ 3. The smallest size of Eastern hard-shell clams.

_____ 4. The largest size of Eastern hard-shell clams.

_____ 5. In bivalves (animals with a pair of hinged shells), the muscle that closes the shells.

_____ 6. The pale green liver of a lobster.

_____ 7. The largest of the crabs.

_____ 8. The roe or eggs of a lobster.

_____ 9. The inactive, dying lobster.

_____ 10. The words that the abbreviation IQF stands for.

_____

_____

_____ 11. Market term for raw shrimp in the shell.

_____ 12. A blue crab that was harvested just after it molted or shed its shell.

_____ 13. The words that the abbreviation PDC, as applied to shrimp, stands for.

_____

_____

_____ 14. Coated with a thin layer of ice when frozen, in order to prevent drying.

_____ 15. A fresh-water shellfish that looks like a small lobster.

_____ 16. A small relative of the rock lobster, sometimes sold as rock shrimp.

B. Fin Fish: Market Forms

In the blanks, write the name of the market form that corresponds to the description and illustration.

1. _____ Viscera removed

2. _____ Boneless side of fish

3. _____ Completely intact, as caught

4. _____ Cross-section slices

5. _____ Viscera, scales, head, tail, and fins removed

6. _____ Both sides of fish joined, bones removed

C. Fat Fish and Lean Fish

In the blank before the name of each fish, write the word "lean" if the fish is low in fat; write the word "fat" if it is high in fat.

1. _____ Haddock

2. _____ Salmon

3. _____ Ocean perch

4. _____ Red snapper

5. _____ Tuna

6. _____ Swordfish

7. _____ Pompano

8. _____ Pike

9. _____ Shad

10. _____ Whiting

11. _____ Whitefish

12. _____ Flounder

13. _____ Sole

14. _____ Cod

15. _____ Trout

16. _____ Halibut

17. _____ Bluefish

18. _____ Mackerel

19. _____ Tilefish

20. _____ Monkfish

D. Review: Freshness and Storage

1. List five signs of freshness in whole fin fish.

    (a) _____

    (b) _____

    (c) _____

    (d) _____

    (e) _____

2. What is the most important sign of freshness in fish fillets?

    _____

3. What is the most important sign of freshness in lobsters?

    _____

4. What is the most important sign of freshness in clams, oysters, and mussels? _____

    _____

5. What is the best way to store whole fin fish?

    _____

6. At what temperature should frozen fish be stored?

    _____

7. What is the best way to thaw frozen fish? _____

    _____

8. What is the best way to store fresh clams and oysters in the shell? _____

    _____

9. What are two ways of storing live lobsters?

(a) _____

(b) _____

10. What is the best way to store thawed raw shrimp in the shell?

_____

E. True/False

T   F   **1.** Haddock is an example of flatfish.

T   F   **2.** In general, fat fish are better suited for broiling than lean fish are.

T   F   **3.** In fish cookery, moist-heat methods are used primarily to tenderize tough fish.

T   F   **4.** Some canned fish products are inspected for wholesomeness by the federal government.

T   F   **5.** Shrimp that are designated "21/25" weigh about 1¼ oz each.

T   F   **6.** A fish that is very fresh has clear, white gills.

T   F   **7.** The largest varieties of scallops are called sea scallops.

T   F   **8.** Frozen fish fillets must be completely thawed before they can be breaded.

T   F   **9.** Scallops are available only in the fall, winter, and spring.

T   F   **10.** If baked clams are tough, it is because they weren't cooked long enough.

COOKING FISH AND SHELLFISH

This chapter applies the basic cooking techniques to seafood products. Keeping in mind that the structure of fish is quite different from that of meat and poultry, pay special attention to the ways in which cooking fish differs from cooking meats.

After studying Chapter 15, you should be able to:

1. Cook fish and shellfish by baking.

2. Cook fish and shellfish by broiling.

3. Cook fish and shellfish by sautéing and pan-frying.

4. Cook fish and shellfish by deep-frying.

5. Cook fish and shellfish by poaching and simmering in court bouillon.

6. Cook fish and shellfish by poaching in fumet and wine.

7. Cook fish and shellfish by simmering and steaming.

A. Terms

Fill in each blank with the term that is defined or described.

_____ 1. Water containing seasonings, herbs, and usually an acid, used for cooking fish.

_____ 2. Trout that was alive until cooking time and that turns blue when cooked in water containing an acid such as lemon juice or vinegar.

_____   **3.** Fish dredged in flour, sautéed in butter, and served with a topping of lemon juice, parsley, and browned butter.

_____   **4.** A dish consisting of poached fish on a bed of spinach, topped with Mornay sauce.

_____   **5.** A term referring to fish topped with a rich sauce and browned under a broiler or salamander.

_____   **6.** Mussels steamed with white wine, shallots, and parsley.

_____   **7.** A dish consisting of fish or seafood served in a cream sauce flavored with sherry or other fortified wine.

_____   **8.** A French term meaning "to cook a product in its own juices; to sweat."

_____   **9.** Wrapped in paper for cooking so that the food is steamed in its own moisture.

_____   **10.** Thin, flat items such as fish fillets rolled up into tight rolls, then cooked and served in this fashion.

_____   **11.** French menu name for poached sole in white wine sauce.

_____   **12.** Dish similar to the one described in number 11, but with the addition of mushrooms.

_____   **13.** A dish consisting of trout prepared as described in number 3, but garnished with browned sliced almonds.

_____   **14.** A dish consisting of cut-up lobster sautéed and then cooked and served in a sauce made with tomato, shallot, garlic, white wine, brandy, fish stock, and herbs.

_____   **15.** A style of preparation in which a poached fish or seafood item is served "swimming" in a broth made of its poaching liquid.

B. Review of Poaching Fish in Wine

The following are the steps in the procedure for poaching fish in wine and fish stock, but they are out of order. Place them in the correct order by writing the number "1" in front of the first step, "2" in front of the second step, and so on.

_____ Butter the bottom of the pan.

_____ Reduce the poaching liquid to about one-fourth of its volume.

_____ Strain the sauce.

_____ Sprinkle chopped shallots into the pan.

_____ Add enough fish fumet and white wine to almost cover the fish.

_____ Collect all equipment and food supplies.

_____ Plate the fish and coat with the sauce.

_____ Cover the fish and bring the liquid to a simmer.

_____ Arrange the fish portions in the pan in a single layer. Season them lightly.

_____ Poach the fish, covered, in the oven or on the range at moderate heat.

_____ Add fish velouté and heavy cream. Bring to a simmer and season with salt, white pepper, and lemon juice.

_____ Drain the poaching liquid into another pan. Keep the fish warm.

C. Short-Answer Questions

1. When you are sautéing a fillet of fish, which side of the fillet should be browned first? _____

_____ .

2. The breading on deep-fried fish serves several purposes. List three purposes.

   (a) _____

   (b) _____

   (c) _____

3. Besides mirepoix and various seasonings, herbs, and spices, the two main ingredients in a court bouillon

   for cooking fish are _____ and _____ .

4. Plain fish steaks to be baked or broiled are usually coated with _____ before cooking.

5. What is the normal oven temperature range for baking fish? _____

6. The main flavoring ingredient for scampi-style broiled shrimp is _____ .

7. Whole fish to be served cold on a buffet are usually cooked by what method? _____

8. When you are rolling up sole fillets to prepare them for cooking, which side of the fillet should be on the

   inside of the roll? _____

9. The preferred fats for sautéing fish are oil and _____ .

10. Fish to be sautéed à la meunière is often soaked in _____ before dredging it in

    _____ . This helps form a crust that browns nicely.

D. Recipe Conversion

The following ingredients and quantities are for a Baked Clam recipe that yields 10 portions at 3 clams each. Convert the recipe to the yields indicated.

	10 portions, 3 clams each	30 portions, 3 clams each	30 portions, 4 clams each
Cherrystone clams	30		
Olive oil	2 oz		
Shallots	1½ oz		
Garlic, chopped	1 tsp		
Lemon juice	5 tsp		
Bread crumbs, fresh	10 oz		
Chopped parsley	1 tbsp		
Oregano	¾ tsp		
White pepper	⅛ tsp		
Parmesan cheese	⅓ cup		
Lemon wedges	10		

Recipe Conversion—Metric

The following ingredients and quantities are for a Baked Clam recipe that yields 10 portions at 3 clams each. Convert the recipe to the yields indicated.

	10 portions, 3 clams each	30 portions, 3 clams each	30 portions, 4 clams each
Cherrystone clams	30		
Olive oil	60 mL		
Shallots	50 g		
Garlic, chopped	5 mL		
Lemon juice	25 mL		
Bread crumbs, fresh	300 g		
Chopped parsley	15 mL		
Oregano	3 mL		
White pepper	0.5 mL		
Parmesan cheese	75 mL		
Lemon wedges	10		

E. Portion Cost

Cost out the following recipe. For prices of the ingredients, use figures supplied by your instructor or the *Sample Prices* on pages 223–224.

ITEM: **POACHED SOLE FILLETS BONNE FEMME**

Ingredient	Recipe Quantity	AP Quantity	Price	Total Amount
Sole fillets	6¼ lb	_____	_____	_____
Butter	7 oz	_____	_____	_____
Flour	4 oz	_____	_____	_____
Fish stock	3 cups	_____	_____	_____
Shallots*	3 oz	_____	_____	_____
Mushrooms*	1½ lb	_____	_____	_____
Heavy cream	12 oz	_____	_____	_____

Total cost _____

Number of portions 25

Cost per portion _____

Note: Remember that you need AP weights of all ingredients (see pages 80 and 84 in the text). Let's assume that you kept a record of the quantities needed when you made this recipe:

To get 3 oz EP shallots, you needed 4 oz AP.

To get 1½ lb EP mushrooms, you needed 1 lb 10 oz AP.

Portion Cost—Metric

Cost out the following recipe. For prices of the ingredients, use figures supplied by your instructor or the *Sample Prices* on pages 223–224.

ITEM: **POACHED SOLE FILLETS BONNE FEMME**

Ingredient	Recipe Quantity	AP Quantity	Price	Total Amount
Sole fillets	3 kg	_____	_____	_____
Butter	200 g	_____	_____	_____
Flour	125 g	_____	_____	_____
Fish stock	750 mL	_____	_____	_____
Shallots*	100 g	_____	_____	_____
Mushrooms*	700 g	_____	_____	_____
Heavy cream	350 mL	_____	_____	_____
			Total cost	_____
			Number of portions	25
			Cost per portion	_____

Note: Remember that you need AP weights of all ingredients (see pages 80 and 84 in the text). Let's assume that you kept a record of the quantities needed when you made this recipe:

To get 100 g EP shallots, you needed 125 g AP.

To get 700 g EP mushrooms, you needed 750 g AP.

UNDERSTANDING VEGETABLES

The material on vegetables and starches is divided into three chapters. While each of these three chapters of exercises is relatively short, together they contain many important points to study and review.

After studying Chapter 16, you should be able to:

1. Control texture, flavor, color, and nutritional changes when cooking vegetables.

2. Prepare and serve vegetables cooked to their proper doneness.

3. Judge quality in cooked vegetables, based on color, appearance, texture, flavor, seasonings, and appropriateness of combination with sauces or other vegetables.

4. Perform prepreparation for fresh vegetables.

5. Calculate yields based on trimming losses.

6. Check quality of frozen, canned, and dried vegetables.

A. Terms

Fill in each blank with the term that is defined or described.

_____   **1.** Compounds that give vegetables their color.

_____   **2.** Firm to the bite, not soft or mushy; a term used to describe the texture of vegetables and some other foods that are cooked to this stage of doneness.

_____   **3.** The compound that colors green vegetables green.

_____   **4.** The weight of the solids, minus the juice, in a can of vegetables or fruits.

_____   **5.** The size of the individual pieces in a can of vegetables (for example, the diameter of the peas in a can).

_____   **6.** The compounds that color carrots and sweet potatoes orange.

_____   **7.** The compounds that color tomatoes and red peppers red.

_____   **8.** The compounds that color corn yellow.

_____   **9.** The compounds that color beets and red cabbage red.

_____   **10.** The compounds that color cauliflower and potatoes white.

_____   **11.** The fuzzy center of an artichoke.

_____   **12.** Dried, discolored spots on frozen foods due to improper storage or packaging.

_____   **13.** A kitchen procedure that involves dividing a large quantity of a food item into several smaller containers and cooking each one separately as needed.

_____   **14.** A kitchen procedure that involves partially cooking foods ahead of time, refrigerating them, then finishing portions of the foods as needed at service time.

B. Short-Answer Questions

1. If green beans are cooked with lemon juice, their color will turn _____ .

2. When peas are harvested, their _____ content begins to change to starch.

3. Frozen vegetables should be stored at a temperature of _____ .

4. Baking soda added to cooking water makes the texture of vegetables _____ .

5. Cut surfaces of artichokes are rubbed with _____ so that they will not turn brown.

6. Rutabagas should be cooked uncovered so that _____

_____

7. The top of a can of vegetables should be _____ before it is opened

8. A bulging can of green beans should be _____ .

9. Vitamins in vegetables, can be lost or destroyed by

(a) _____ , (b) _____ ,

(c) _____ , (d) _____ ,

(e) _____ , and (f) _____ .

10. Vegetables should be cut into neat, uniform shapes for better appearance and for _____ .

11. When fresh peas are added to cooking water, the temperature of the water should be _____ .

12. The bottom portions of asparagus stalks are _____ so that the asparagus will cook more evenly.

13. After they are picked over and cleaned, most dried beans are _____ before they are cooked, to shorten cooking time.

14. Frozen vegetables need less cooking time than fresh vegetables because _____ .

15. Two or more batches of cooked vegetables should not be mixed together because _____

_____ .

C. Math Exercise: Trimming Loss

The exercises below are of two kinds, calculating yield and calculating amount needed. To do the calculations, you need to know the percentage yield for each vegetable, as listed in Table 16.2 of the text. For your convenience, the necessary percentages are repeated here.

Artichokes, Jerusalem	80%
Asparagus	55%
Beans, green	88%
Broccoli	70%
Cabbage	80%
Celery	75%
Eggplant	75% (peeled)

Kohlrabi	55%
Leeks	50%
Mushrooms	90%
Okra	82%
Onions, dry	90%
Peas	40%
Potatoes	80%
Turnips	75%
Zucchini	90%

Calculating Amount Needed

Assume you need the following quantities, EP, of the indicated fresh vegetables. Calculate the AP weight you will need to get the required yield. (Questions 1–10 use U.S. measures; questions 11–20 use metric measures. Answer whichever questions are assigned by your instructor.)

	EP Weight Desired	AP Weight Needed
1. Kohlrabi	1 lb	_____
2. Potatoes	12 oz	_____
3. Jerusalem artichokes	1 lb	_____
4. Eggplant, peeled	2½ lb	_____
5. Leeks	6 oz	_____
6. Okra	8 oz	_____
7. Onions, dry	1½ lb	_____
8. Mushrooms	1 lb	_____
9. Celery	3 lb	_____
10. Zucchini	2 lb	_____

	EP Weight Desired	AP Weight Needed
11. Kohlrabi	500 g	_____
12. Potatoes	400 g	_____
13. Jerusalem artichokes	450 g	_____
14. Eggplant, peeled	1.25 kg	_____
15. Leeks	200 g	_____
16. Okra	250 g	_____
17. Onions, dry	700 g	_____
18. Mushrooms	475 g	_____
19. Celery	1.5 kg	_____
20. Zucchini	900 g	_____

Calculating Yield

Assume you have the following quantities, AP, of the indicated fresh vegetables. Calculate the EP weight you will have left after trimming. (Questions 21–30 use U.S. measures; questions 31–40 use metric measures. Answer whichever questions are assigned by your instructor.)

	AP Weight	EP Weight
21. Asparagus	12 oz	_____
22. Red cabbage	6 lb	_____
23. Mushrooms	2½ lb	_____
24. Green beans	1½ lb	_____
25. Peas	4½ lb	_____
26. Turnips	2 lb	_____
27. Broccoli	2½ lb	_____
28. Leeks	6 lb	_____
29. Okra	1 lb	_____
30. Zucchini	5 lb	_____
31. Asparagus	375 g	_____
32. Red cabbage	3 kg	_____
33. Mushrooms	1.25 kg	_____

34. Green beans   700 g   _____

35. Peas   2.2 kg   _____

36. Turnips   450 g   _____

37. Broccoli   1.2 kg   _____

38. Leeks   2.75 kg   _____

39. Okra   500 g   _____

40. Zucchini   2.75 kg   _____

COOKING VEGETABLES

This chapter continues your review of vegetables, concentrating on cooking techniques. After studying Chapter 17, you should be able to:

1. Cook vegetables by boiling and steaming.
2. Cook vegetables by sautéing and pan-frying.
3. Cook vegetables by braising.
4. Cook vegetables by baking.
5. Cook vegetables by broiling.
6. Cook vegetables by deep-frying.

A. Terms

Fill in each blank with the term that is defined or described.

_____ 1. A style of vegetable preparation in which the vegetables are topped with browned sliced almonds.

_____ 2. A style of vegetable preparation in which the vegetable preparation is covered with a topping, such as a sauce, cheese, and/or bread crumbs, and browned under a boiler or salamander.

_____ 3. A dish consisting of braised sauerkraut served with a variety of sausages and other pork products.

_____ 4. A general term referring to foods coated with or mixed with a batter and deep-fried.

_____ 5. To give a vegetable a shiny coating by cooking it with sugar and butter or with a syrup.

_____ 6. Thick vegetable purées or mixtures of small pieces of vegetable and a heavy béchamel or other binder, formed into shapes, breaded, and fried.

_____ 7. A style of vegetable preparation in which the vegetable is topped with chopped hard-cooked egg, chopped parsley, and bread crumbs browned in butter.

_____ 8. A vegetable stew made of eggplant, tomatoes, onions, peppers, and zucchini.

_____ 9. Artichoke bottoms filled with peas.

_____ 10. A coarse paste or hash made of finely chopped mushrooms sautéed with shallots.

_____ 11. Peas cooked with pearl onions and shredded lettuce in a lightly bound white stock.

B. True/False

T　F　　1. One advantage of cooking vegetables in a pressure steamer is that the door can be opened at any time to check on the vegetables.

T　F　　2. Simmering is better than boiling for vegetables that can be easily broken.

T　F　　3. If green peas are not to be served soon after they are boiled, they should be cooled in cold water and refrigerated until needed.

T　F　　4. Zucchini must be parboiled before being sautéed.

T　F　　5. Sautéing is similar to pan-frying, except that sautéing always requires more fat.

T　F　　6. To sauté vegetables, set the sauté pan over moderate heat, add the butter and vegetables, then wait until the pan gets hot before flipping the vegetables.

T　F　　7. Braised vegetables are browned in fat, then cooked slowly in a small amount of liquid.

T　F　　8. The difference between braised meat and braised vegetables is that mirepoix is never used with vegetables.

T　F　　9. Vinegar is added to braised red cabbage to flavor it and to enhance its red color.

T　F　　10. Quick-cooking vegetables are best for broiling.

T　F　　11. All vegetables that are coated in batter and deep-fried must first be blanched or parboiled.

T　F　　12. Deep-fried vegetables are best if cooked to order.

T　F　　13. Perforated pans should never be used for steaming vegetables, because too many juices will be lost.

T　F　　14. Creamed spinach is made by cooking fresh spinach in a cream sauce.

C. Recipe Conversion

The following ingredients and quantities are for a Braised Red Cabbage recipe that yields 25 portions at 5 oz each. Convert the recipe to the yields indicated.

	25 portions, 5 oz each	10 portions, 5 oz each	15 portions, 4 oz each
Red cabbage, AP	6 lb		
Bacon	12 oz		
Onions	1 lb		
Sugar	1 oz		
White stock	1½ pt		
Apples, cored and diced	1 lb		
Cloves	4		
Whole allspice	6		
Stick cinnamon	1 piece		
Red wine vinegar	4 oz		
Red wine	1 cup		
Salt	to taste		
Pepper	to taste		

Recipe Conversion—Metric

The following ingredients and quantities are for a Braised Red Cabbage recipe that yields 25 portions at 125 g each. Convert the recipe to the yields indicated.

	25 portions, 125 g each	10 portions, 125 g each	15 portions, 100 g each
Red cabbage, AP	2.5 kg		
Bacon	350 g		
Onions	400 g		
Sugar	25 g		
White stock	700 mL		
Apples, cored and diced	400 g		
Cloves	4		
Whole allspice	6		
Stick cinnamon	1 piece		
Red wine vinegar	100 mL		
Red wine	250 mL		
Salt	to taste		
Pepper	to taste		

D. Portion Cost

Cost out the following recipes. For prices of the ingredients, use figures supplied by your instructor or the *Sample Prices* on pages 223–224.

ITEM: ARTICHOKES CLAMART

Ingredient	Recipe Quantity	AP Quantity	Price	Total Amount
Artichokes	10	_____	_____	_____
Lemons	2	_____	_____	_____
Flour	1 oz	_____	_____	_____
Cold water	3 pt	_____	_____	_____
Salt	½ oz	_____	_____	_____
Peas, frozen	10 oz	_____	_____	_____
Butter	3 oz	_____	_____	_____
			Total cost	_____
			Number of portions	10
			Cost per portion	_____

ITEM: GLAZED CARROTS

Ingredient	Recipe Quantity	AP Quantity	Price	Total Amount
Carrots, AP	6½ lb	_____	_____	_____
Butter	3 oz	_____	_____	_____
Sugar	2 oz	_____	_____	_____
			Total cost	_____
			Number of portions	25
			Cost per portion	_____

ITEM: PUREED BUTTERNUT SQUASH

Ingredient	Recipe Quantity	AP Quantity	Price	Total Amount
Butternut squash	10 lb	_____	_____	_____
Butter	8 oz	_____	_____	_____
Brown sugar	4 oz	_____	_____	_____
Salt	½ oz	_____	_____	_____
			Total cost	_____
			Number of portions	25
			Cost per portion	_____

Portion Cost—Metric

Cost out the following recipes. For prices of the ingredients, use figures supplied by your instructor or the *Sample Prices* on pages 223–224.

ITEM: ARTICHOKES CLAMART

Ingredient	Recipe Quantity	AP Quantity	Price	Total Amount
Artichokes	10	_____	_____	_____
Lemons	2	_____	_____	_____
Flour	30 g	_____	_____	_____
Cold water	1.5 l	_____	_____	_____
Salt	15 g	_____	_____	_____
Peas, frozen	300 g	_____	_____	_____
Butter	90 g	_____	_____	_____
			Total cost	_____
			Number of portions	10
			Cost per portion	_____

ITEM: **GLAZED CARROTS**

Ingredient	Recipe Quantity	AP Quantity	Price	Total Amount
Carrots, AP	3 kg	_____	_____	_____
Butter	100 g	_____	_____	_____
Sugar	60 g	_____	_____	_____
			Total cost	_____
			Number of portions	25
			Cost per portion	_____

ITEM: **PUREED BUTTERNUT SQUASH**

Ingredient	Recipe Quantity	AP Quantity	Price	Total Amount
Butternut squash	5 kg	_____	_____	_____
Butter	250 g	_____	_____	_____
Brown sugar	125 g	_____	_____	_____
Salt	15 g	_____	_____	_____
			Total cost	_____
			Number of portions	25
			Cost per portion	_____

POTATOES AND OTHER STARCHES

The last of three chapters covering basic vegetable cookery, this unit concentrates on potatoes and on other starchy products such as rice and pasta. The importance of potatoes and starches in our diet suggests that a thorough review of this material is important.

After studying Chapter 18, you should be able to:

1. Distinguish the major types of potatoes and the best uses for each.
2. Select potatoes of high quality and store them properly.
3. Cook potatoes by boiling and steaming, and prepare potato purée.
4. Cook potatoes by baking, sautéing, pan-frying, and deep-frying.
5. Distinguish the major types of rice.
6. Prepare rice by boiling and steaming and by the pilaf and risotto methods.
7. Distinguish major kinds and shapes of commercial pasta, and determine their quality.
8. Prepare fresh and commercial pasta products.

A. Terms

Fill in each blank with the term that is defined or described.

_____ 1. A variety of potato, often from Idaho, having a high starch content and often used for baking.

_____ 2. Rice that is first cooked in fat, then in liquid; braised rice.

_____ 3. Firm, not soft or mushy, to the bite; a term often used to describe the doneness of pasta.

_____ 4. A variety of short-grain rice from Italy.

_____ 5. General term for potatoes that are low in starch and high in sugar, with a firm, moist texture.

_____ 6. A poisonous substance present in the green parts found in some potatoes.

_____ 7. A long-grain rice from India, with a unique nutty flavor.

_____ 8. A type of Asian short-grain rice that becomes quite sticky and chewy when cooked.

_____ 9. A type of cracked wheat that has been partially cooked; often used in salads.

_____ 10. An Italian rice dish made by adding stock a little at a time to rice in a pan and stirring constantly as it cooks.

_____ 11. Rice with the bran left on.

_____ 12. High-gluten flour used for the best-quality commercial macaroni products.

_____ 13. Baked casserole made of wide, flat noodles layered with other products such as tomato sauce and cheese.

_____ 14. A paste made of fresh basil and other ingredients, often used as a pasta sauce.

_____ 15. Pillow-shaped stuffed egg noodles.

B. Classic Potato Preparations

Column 1 below is a list of descriptions of various classic potato dishes. Column 2 is a list of the names of these dishes. Match the names to the descriptions by writing the letter of the correct name in the space before the description.

_____ 1. Potato purée combined with butter and egg yolks, often used for decorative work

_____ 2. Sliced potatoes baked with cream, milk, and cheese

_____ 3. Cooked potatoes chopped, formed into cakes, and pan-fried

_____ 4. Trimmed potatoes simmered in stock with onion and carrot

_____ 5. Mixture of duchesse potatoes and pâte à choux, deep-fried

_____ 6. Small tournéed potatoes browned in butter

_____ 7. Thin, matchstick-sized french fries

_____ 8. Plain boiled potatoes

_____ 9. Same as number 5 but flavored with parmesan cheese

_____ 10. Cut with ball cutter and browned in butter

_____ 11. Sliced potatoes arranged in overlapping rings in a pan and baked with butter

_____ 12. Sliced potatoes and onions moistened with stock and baked with roast lamb

_____ 13. Baked in cheese sauce until browned on top

_____ 14. Duchesse mixture shaped, breaded, and deep-fried

_____ 15. Sliced, boiled potatoes pan-fried with onions

_____ 16. Diced potatoes pan-fried with bacon, onion, green pepper, and pimiento

_____ 17. Steamed potatoes

_____ 18. Baked potatoes puréed with butter, made into cakes, and pan-fried

_____ 19. Boiled potatoes sliced and pan-fried

_____ 20. Potatoes sliced on a mandoline into waffle shapes, deep-fried until crisp

a. Rissolé or Cocotte
b. Dauphine Potatoes
c. Parisienne or Noisette
d. Duchesse Potatoes
e. au Gratin
f. Boulangère
g. Home Fries
h. O'Brien
i. Croquettes
j. Lyonnaise
k. Hashed Browns
l. Allumette
m. Dauphinoise
n. Anna
o. Bouillon
p. Gaufrette
q. Macaire
r. Pommes Vapeurs
s. Lorette
t. Pommes Natures

C. Short-Answer Questions

1. List six characteristics of a high-quality potato.

   (a) _____

   (b) _____

   (c) _____

   (d) _____

   (e) _____

   (f) _____

2. At what temperature should potatoes be stored? _____

3. The following are steps in the procedure for making potato purée for duchesse potatoes. Fill in the missing step.

   (a) Wash, peel, and eye. Cut into uniform sizes.

   (b) Simmer until tender.

   (c) Drain in colander.

   (d) _____

   (e) Pass through a food mill to purée.

4. How are french fries blanched? _____

   _____

   _____

5. Why should starchy potatoes not be refrigerated? _____

   _____

6. What is parboiled rice? _____

   _____

7. Which kind of rice is most often used as a side dish—short grain, medium grain, or long grain? _____

8. If you are making pilaf with 1 qt (or 1 L) of raw rice, how much stock will you need? _____

9. To cook 1 lb of spaghetti, how much water do you need? _____

10. To get three 10-oz portions (or, if you use metric units, three 300-g portions) of cooked spaghetti, about how much dry, commercial spaghetti do you need? _____

D. Pasta Shapes

In the space before the name of each pasta shape, write the letter of the illustration that corresponds.

_____ 1. Fusilli

_____ 2. Ditalini

_____ 3. Spaghettini

_____ 4. Lasagne

_____ 5. Penne

_____ 6. Orzo

_____ 7. Stelline

_____ 8. Ziti

_____ 9. Conchiglie

_____ 10. Elbow macaroni

_____ 11. Fettuccine

_____ 12. Manicotti

E. Recipe Conversion

The following ingredients and quantities are for a recipe for Hungarian Potatoes, yielding 25 portions, 4 oz each. Convert the recipe to the yields indicated.

	25 portions, 4 oz each	15 portions, 4 oz each	15 portions, 5 oz each
Butter	4 oz		
Onion	8 oz		
Paprika	2 tsp		
Tomato concassée	1 lb		
Potatoes, peeled	5 lb		
Chicken stock	1 qt		
Salt	to taste		
Pepper	to taste		
Chopped parsley	½ cup		

The following ingredients and quantities are for a recipe for Pesto, yielding 12 portions at 2 oz each. Convert the recipe to the yields indicated.

	12 portions, 2 oz each	4 portions, 2 oz each	16 portions, 1½ oz each
Fresh basil leaves	2 qt		
Olive oil	1½ cups		
Pignoli	2 oz		
Garlic cloves	6		
Salt	1½ tsp		
Parmesan cheese	5 oz		
Romano cheese	1½ oz		

Recipe Conversion—Metric

The following ingredients and quantities are for a recipe for Hungarian Potatoes, yielding 25 portions at 100 g each. Convert the recipe to the yields indicated.

	25 portions, 100 g each	15 portions, 100 g each	15 portions, 125 g each
Butter	100 g		
Onion	200 g		
Paprika	10 mL		
Tomato concassée	400 g		
Potatoes, peeled	2 kg		
Chicken stock	800 mL		
Salt	to taste		
Pepper	to taste		
Chopped parsley	100 mL		

The following ingredients and quantities are for a recipe for Pesto, yielding 12 portions at 60 mL each. Convert the recipe to the yields indicated.

	12 portions, 60 mL each	4 portions, 60 mL each	16 portions, 45 mL each
Fresh basil leaves	2 L		
Olive oil	375 mL		
Pignoli	60 g		
Garlic cloves	6		
Salt	7 mL		
Parmesan cheese	150 g		
Romano cheese	45 g		

F. Portion Cost

Cost out the following recipes. For prices of the ingredients, use figures supplied by your instructor or the *Sample Prices* on pages 223–224.

ITEM: **BOULANGERE POTATOES**

Ingredient	Recipe Quantity	AP Quantity	Price	Total Amount
Onions, AP	2½ lb	_____	_____	_____
Butter	5 oz	_____	_____	_____
Potatoes, all-purpose, AP	7½ lb	_____	_____	_____
Chicken stock	1 qt	_____	_____	_____
			Total cost	_____
			Number of portions	25
			Cost per portion	_____

ITEM: **FETTUCCINE ALFREDO**

Ingredient	Recipe Quantity	AP Quantity	Price	Total Amount
Fresh pasta				
Flour	1 lb	_____	_____	_____
Eggs	5	_____	_____	_____
Olive oil	½ oz	_____	_____	_____
Heavy cream	1 pt	_____	_____	_____
Butter	2 oz	_____	_____	_____
Parmesan cheese	6 oz	_____	_____	_____
			Total cost	_____
			Number of portions	10
			Cost per portion	_____

Portion Cost—Metric

Cost out the following recipes. For prices of the ingredients, use figures supplied by your instructor or the *Sample Prices* on pages 223–224.

ITEM: **BOULANGERE POTATOES**

Ingredient	Recipe Quantity	AP Quantity	Price	Total Amount
Onions, AP	1.2 kg	————	————	————
Butter	150 g	————	————	————
Potatoes, all-purpose, AP	3.6 kg	————	————	————
Chicken stock	1 L	————	————	————
			Total cost	————
			Number of portions	25
			Cost per portion	————

ITEM: **FETTUCCINE ALFREDO**

Ingredient	Recipe Quantity	AP Quantity	Price	Total Amount
Fresh pasta				
Flour	450 g	————	————	————
Eggs	5	————	————	————
Olive oil	15 mL	————	————	————
Heavy cream	500 mL	————	————	————
Butter	60 g	————	————	————
Parmesan cheese	175 g	————	————	————
			Total cost	————
			Number of portions	10
			Cost per portion	————

SALADS AND SALAD DRESSINGS

Although some of the preparations in this chapter involve cooking, most of our attention is on foods that are served and eaten raw. Emphasis is on product understanding and on careful preparation. After studying Chapter 19, you should be able to:

1. Describe the different salad types and select appropriate salad recipes for use as appetizer, accompaniment, main course, separate course, and dessert salads.

2. Identify salad greens and other salad ingredients.

3. Judge quality and do preparation of fresh fruits.

4. Identify the parts of a salad.

5. Assemble salads that have eye appeal.

6. Set up an efficient system for producing salads in quantity.

7. Produce green salads, vegetable salads, cooked salads, fruit salads, combination salads, and gelatin salads, and set up a salad bar.

8. Identify salad dressing ingredients.

9. Produce oil and vinegar dressings, mayonnaise and mayonnaise-based dressings, cooked dressing, and specialty dressings.

A. Terms

Fill in each blank with the term that is defined or described.

_____ 1. A red-leafed, Italian variety of chickory.

_____ 2. A salad mixed with a heavy dressing, such as mayonnaise, to hold it together.

_____ 3. A famous salad made of romaine lettuce and a dressing made of olive oil, lemon juice, eggs, garlic, and anchovies.

_____ 4. To soak a food in a seasoned liquid to give it flavor and moistness.

_____ 5. A dark brown vinegar that has been aged in wooden barrels.

_____ 6. Oil that has been treated so that it will stay clear and liquid when refrigerated.

_____ 7. The best grade of olive oil, made from the first pressing of olives.

_____ 8. A brand of sheep's-milk cheese made only in a specific region of France.

_____ 9. A uniform mixture of two unmixable liquids.

_____ 10. A salad dressing made of oil, vinegar, and seasonings.

_____ 11. Having a smooth scar on the stem end of a melon, with no trace of stem.

_____ 12. A classic salad made of apples, celery, and walnuts, with a mayonnaise-based dressing.

B. True/False

T   F   1. Luncheon salads served as a main course must always contain a meat or seafood item.

T   F   2. The four basic parts of a salad are the underliner, the base, the lettuce, and the garnish.

T   F   3. The dressing should be added to a green salad at least a half hour before service, so that the flavors have time to blend.

T   F   4. Cutting ingredients neatly is one way to enhance the appearance of a salad.

T   F   5. In general, salad ingredients should be in bite-sized pieces.

T   F   6. The purpose of garnish is to make a salad more attractive to the eye.

T   F   7. Peaches, pears, and pineapples are examples of fruits that will discolor when cut and exposed to air.

T   F   8. Boston lettuce is often tough and bitter, so it is not used by itself in green salads.

T   F   9. Watercress is used mainly as a garnish and is inappropriate in mixed green salads.

T   F   **10.** Moisture is necessary to maintain crispness in salad greens.

T   F   **11.** Cooked vegetables to be used in salads must always be cooked until very tender.

T   F   **12.** Raw ingredients should never be added to cooked salads.

T   F   **13.** To prevent food-borne disease, the ingredients of a mayonnaise-based salad must be cold when they are combined.

T   F   **14.** Dressings for fruit salads should never be sweetened, so that they will counteract the sweetness of the fruit.

C. Gelatin Review

1. Gelatin dissolves in water at about _____ degrees Fahrenheit (or _____ degrees Celsius).

2. To avoid lumping, plain gelatin is first mixed with _____.

3. To use a flavored gelatin sweetened with sugar, you need _____ ounces of gelatin mix per gallon of water (or _____ grams of gelatin mix per liter of water).

4. Basic proportions for unflavored gelatin are _____ ounces of dry gelatin per gallon of liquid (or _____ grams per liter).

5. The setting power of gelatin is weakened by _____, by _____, and by _____. Therefore, most gelatin salads need more gelatin than the basic proportion indicated in number 4.

6. To dissolve sweetened, flavored gelatin, stir it into _____ water.

7. _____ and _____ are two examples of fresh fruits that should not be added to gelatin.

8. The proper time to mix solid ingredients into gelatin is _____.

9. In the space below, write out the basic procedure for unmolding gelatin.

_____

_____

_____

_____

_____

_____

_____

_____

D. Salad Dressing Review

1. The two main ingredients of most standard salad dressings are _____ and _____. Other ingredients, such as seasonings, herbs, and egg yolks, are added to modify flavor and texture.

2. _____ is an all-purpose blend of oils that can be used for a wide variety of dressings because of its neutral flavor.

3. Five examples of different vinegars that can be used to make salad dressings are:

    _____

    _____

    _____

    _____

    _____

4. To make a basic oil and vinegar dressing, you need _____ pint(s) of oil for each pint of vinegar.

5. The most important thickening agent in cooked dressing is _____, while the ingredient that

    makes mayonnaise thick is _____.

6. So that the dressing will not be too acidic, a vinegar that contains more than 5% acid may have to be

    _____ before being included in the dressing.

7. Suggest one ingredient that can be substituted for oil to make a low-fat vinaigrette. _____

8. In the space below, explain how to make mayonnaise. Be sure to include all necessary steps, and number the steps to make the procedure easier to read. Include ingredient quantities if your instructor asks you to do so.

    _____

    _____

    _____

    _____

    _____

    _____

E. Math Exercise: Trimming Loss

The exercises below are of two kinds, calculating yield and calculating amount needed. To do the calculations, you need to know the percentage yield for each fruit, as listed in Table 19.1 of the text. For your convenience, the necessary percentages are repeated here.

Apples	75%	Papayas	65%
Bananas	70%	Peaches	75%
Kiwi fruit	80%	Pears	75%
Mangoes	75%	Pineapples	50%
Oranges (sectioned)	65%	Watermelon	45%

Calculating Amount Needed

Assume you need the following quantities, EP (edible portion, with no peels, pits, cores, or stems), of the indicated fresh fruits. Calculate the AP weight you will need to get the required yield. (Questions 1–7 use U.S. measures; questions 8–14 use metric measures. Answer whichever questions are assigned by your instructor.)

	EP Weight Desired	AP Weight Needed
1. Bananas	12 oz	_____
2. Apples	2 lb	_____
3. Peaches	3 lb	_____
4. Oranges (sectioned)	½ lb	_____
5. Kiwi fruit	6 oz	_____
6. Pineapple	8 oz	_____
7. Papaya	1½ lb	_____
8. Bananas	350 g	_____
9. Apples	1 kg	_____
10. Peaches	1.5 kg	_____
11. Oranges (sections)	250 g	_____
12. Kiwi fruit	175 g	_____
13. Pineapple	250 g	_____
14. Papaya	750 g	_____

Calculating Yield

Assume you have the following quantities, AP, of the indicated fresh fruits. Calculate the EP weight you will have left after trimming, peeling, coring, etc. (Questions 15–21 use U.S. measures; questions 22–28 use metric measures. Answer whichever questions are assigned by your instructor.)

	AP Weight	**EP Weight**
15. Pears	3½ lb	_____
16. Bananas	6 lb	_____
17. Mangoes	2½ lb	_____
18. Watermelon	4½ lb	_____
19. Kiwi fruit	1 lb	_____
20. Apples	2 lb	_____
21. Pineapple	3½ lb	_____
22. Pears	1.6 kg	_____
23. Bananas	3 kg	_____
24. Mangoes	1.2 kg	_____
25. Watermelon	2.3 kg	_____
26. Kiwi fruit	400 g	_____
27. Apples	1 kg	_____
28. Pineapple	1.5 kg	_____

F. Recipe Conversion

The following ingredients and quantities are for a recipe for Cucumbers and Onions in Sour Cream, yielding 25 salads at 3½ oz each. Convert the recipe to the yields indicated.

	25 portions, 3½ oz each	40 portions, 3½ oz each	14 portions, 3 oz each
Cider vinegar	1 pt		
Water	1 cup		
Sugar	1 oz		
Salt	2 tsp		
White pepper	½ tsp		
Cucumbers, peeled	4 lb		
Onions, peeled	1 lb		
Sour cream	1 pt		
Mayonnaise	1 cup		
Lettuce leaves for underliners*	25		

Note: This ingredient is calculated differently from the others. Can you see why?

Recipe Conversion—Metric

The following ingredients and quantities are for a recipe for Cucumbers and Onions in Sour Cream, yielding 25 salads at 100 g each. Convert the recipe to the yields indicated.

	25 portions, 100 g each	**40 portions, 100 g each**	**14 portions, 90 g each**
Cider vinegar	500 mL		
Water	250 mL		
Sugar	30 g		
Salt	10 mL		
White pepper	2 mL		
Cucumbers, peeled	2 kg		
Onions, peeled	500 g		
Sour cream	500 mL		
Mayonnaise	250 mL		
Lettuce leaves for underliners*	25		

Note: This ingredient is calculated differently from the others. Can you see why?

G. Portion Cost

Cost out the following recipe. For prices of the ingredients, use figures supplied by your instructor or the *Sample Prices* on pages 223–224.

ITEM: **CARROT RAISIN SALAD**

Ingredient	Recipe Quantity	AP Quantity	Price	Total Amount
Carrots, AP	5 lb	_____	_____	_____
Raisins	8 oz	_____	_____	_____
Mayonnaise	1½ cups	_____	_____	_____
Salad oil	6 fl oz	_____	_____	_____
Wine vinegar	2 fl oz	_____	_____	_____
Iceberg lettuce	1 head	_____	_____	_____

Total cost _____

Number of portions 25

Cost per portion _____

Portion Cost—Metric

Cost out the following recipe. For prices of the ingredients, use figures supplied by your instructor or the *Sample Prices* on pages 223–224.

ITEM: **CARROT RAISIN SALAD**

Ingredient	Recipe Quantity	AP Quantity	Price	Total Amount
Carrots, AP	2 kg	_____	_____	_____
Raisins	200 g	_____	_____	_____
Mayonnaise	300 mL	_____	_____	_____
Salad oil	150 mL	_____	_____	_____
Wine vinegar	50 mL	_____	_____	_____
Iceberg lettuce	1 head	_____	_____	_____
			Total cost	_____
			Number of portions	25
			Cost per portion	_____

SANDWICHES AND HORS D'OEUVRES

Chapter 20 is a continuation of the cold foods or pantry unit begun in Chapter 19. Although many of these foods, such as sandwiches and canapés, may seem simple at first glance, they exemplify many of the basic principles of professional kitchen production, such as careful and thorough mise en place, well-developed manual skills, and efficient planning and organization of tasks.

After studying Chapter 20, you should be able to:

1. Select, store, and serve fresh, good-quality breads for sandwiches.
2. Use sandwich spreads correctly.
3. List most popular sandwich fillings.
4. Set up a sandwich station.
5. Prepare the major types of sandwiches to order.
6. Prepare sandwiches in quantity.
7. Prepare canapés and other popular hors d'oeuvres.

A. Terms

Fill in each blank with the term that is defined or described.

_____ 1. A sandwich made of corned beef, sauerkraut, Swiss cheese, and Russian dressing on rye bread.

_____ 2. A long, rectangular loaf of bread, often used for sandwiches.

_____ **3.** A bite-sized, open-faced sandwich, served as an hors d'oeuvre.

_____ **4.** French term for raw vegetables, served as hors d'oeuvres.

_____ **5.** A category of hors d'oeuvre that includes raw vegetables (as in number 4) and pickled items.

_____ **6.** A Mexican-style dip made of mashed avocado.

_____ **7.** A sandwich that consists of a filling between two slices of bread.

_____ **8.** A sandwich made of a slice of bread with a topping, but with no top slice of bread.

_____ **9.** A multidecker sandwich made of three slices of toast spread with mayonnaise and filled with sliced chicken or turkey, lettuce, tomato, and bacon.

_____ **10.** A category of appetizer that includes various seafoods or fruits, served cold, usually with a tart or tangy sauce.

_____ **11.** An Italian hors d'oeuvre.

_____ **12.** A small, fancy sandwich, generally made from light, delicate ingredients and bread that has been trimmed of crusts.

B. Sandwich Review

1. List six types of bread that can be used for sandwiches.

    (a) _____

    (b) _____

    (c) _____

    (d) _____

    (e) _____

    (f) _____

2. What are the two most commonly used spreads for sandwiches?

    _____

    _____

3. The following are some basic categories of sandwich filling ingredients. Fill in the blanks with specific examples of each group, naming as many examples as there are spaces.

Beef

(a) _____

(b) _____

(c) _____

(d) _____

(c) _____

(f) _____

Pork and sausage products

(a) _____

(b) _____

(c) _____

(d) _____

(e) _____

(f) _____

(g) _____

Poultry

(a) _____

(b) _____

Fish and shellfish

(a) _____

(b) _____

(c) _____

(d) _____

Cheese

(a) _____

(b) _____

(c) _____

(d) _____

(e) _____

4. List four basic hand tools that are essential on a short-order sandwich station.

(a) _____

(b) _____

(c) _____

(d) _____

5. In the space below, draw a diagram of the proper way to cut a club sandwich.

6. Suppose you are assigned to make a large quantity of turkey sandwiches, using mayonnaise as the spread and lettuce leaves and sliced turkey breast as the filling. In the space below, write out the procedure you would use to prepare the sandwiches efficiently and quickly. Be sure to include all the steps, and number the steps to make the procedure easier to read.

C. Review of Canapé Preparation

1. The three basic parts of a canapé are _____, _____, and _____.

2. In the space below, draw diagrams of three different ways that bread slices can be cut into various shapes for canapés.

3. List four different items that can be used as bases for canapés.

(a) _____

(b) _____

(c) _____

(d) _____

4. What are the two most common types of spreads used for canapés?

_____

_____

5. The following are some basic categories of canapé garnishes. Fill in the blanks with specific examples of each group, naming as many examples as there are spaces.

Fish and shellfish products

(a) _____

(b) _____

(c) _____

(d) _____

(e) _____

(f) _____

(g) _____

(h) _____

Vegetables, pickles, and relishes

(a) _____

(b) _____

(c) _____

(d) _____

(e) _____

(f) _____

(g) _____

(h) _____

(i) _____

(j) _____

Meats

(a) _____

(b) _____

(c) _____

(d) _____

D. Recipe Conversion

The following ingredients and quantities are for a Clam Dip recipe that yields 1 qt. Convert the recipe to the yields indicated.

	1 qt	1½ pt	1 gal
Cream cheese	1 lb 4 oz	_____	_____
Clam juice	3 oz	_____	_____
Dijon-style mustard	2 oz	_____	_____
Worcestershire sauce	1 oz	_____	_____
Horseradish	1 tsp	_____	_____
Grated onion	1½ oz	_____	_____
Hot pepper sauce	½ tsp	_____	_____
Canned clams, drained	12 oz	_____	_____
Salt	to taste	_____	_____
White pepper	to taste	_____	_____

Recipe Conversion—Metric

The following ingredients and quantities are for a Clam Dip recipe that yields 1 L. Convert the recipe to the yields indicated.

	1 L	750 mL	4 L
Cream cheese	625 g	_____	_____
Clam juice	90 g	_____	_____
Dijon-style mustard	60 g	_____	_____
Worcestershire sauce	30 mL	_____	_____
Horseradish	5 mL	_____	_____
Grated onion	45 g	_____	_____
Hot pepper sauce	2 ml	_____	_____
Canned clams, drained	375 g	_____	_____
Salt	to taste	_____	_____
White pepper	to taste	_____	_____

BREAKFAST PREPARATION, DAIRY PRODUCTS, AND COFFEE AND TEA

This chapter discusses cooking techniques for breakfast and dairy items, illustrated by a few typical recipes. In addition, there is a great deal of product information, including a long section on cheese, that may require extra study and review.

After studying Chapter 21, you should be able to:

1. Describe the composition of eggs and the major differences among grades.

2. Store eggs properly.

3. Prepare the following egg items: hard-, medium-, and soft-cooked eggs; poached eggs; fried eggs; shirred eggs; scrambled eggs; omelets; entrée soufflés; and savory custards.

4. Prepare pancakes, waffles, and French toast.

5. Prepare cooked breakfast cereals.

6. Prepare breakfast meats.

7. Describe the major milk, cream, and butter products.

8. Heat and cook with milk without curdling or scorching.

9. Whip cream.

10. Describe the most important kinds of cheese used in American food service.

11. Store and serve cheese properly.

12. Cook with cheese.

13. Prepare coffee and tea.

A. Terms

Fill in each blank with the term that is defined or described.

_____ 1. A dish consisting of poached eggs and Canadian bacon on English muffins, coated with Hollandaise sauce.

_____ 2. Term used to describe fried eggs cooked on one side only.

_____ 3. An egg baked in an individual serving dish, with or without additional ingredients; resembles a fried egg in appearance.

_____ 4. A flat, unfolded omelet consisting of beaten eggs mixed with other ingredients, such as vegetables and meats.

_____ 5. A savory tart consisting of a custard mixture and other ingredients baked in a pastry shell.

_____ 6. Bread dipped into an egg mixture and cooked on a griddle or in a fry pan or deep-fryer.

_____ 7. Milk that has been processed so that the cream doesn't separate out.

_____ 8. Generic term for cheese made with goats' milk.

_____ 9. A manufactured product made of fats and other ingredients, intended to resemble butter.

_____ 10. A dish made of cheddar-type cheese melted with beer and seasonings.

_____ 11. Milk that has been heat-treated to kill disease-causing bacteria.

_____ 12. Milk that has not been heat-treated as in number 11.

_____ 13. A liquid that is thickened or set by the coagulation of egg protein.

_____ 14. A process by which milk proteins coagulate and separate from the whey; in cooking this process is usually undesirable.

_____ 15. A strong, dark coffee made from beans roasted until they are almost black.

_____ 16. Tea that has been fermented by allowing the freshly harvested leaves to oxidize in a damp place.

_____ 17. Tea that has been dried without the fermenting procedure described in number 16.

_____ 18. Tea that has been only partially fermented, so that it has a greenish-brown color.

_____ 19. A term meaning "half-cup," referring to strong, dark coffee served in small cups after dinner.

_____ 20. A dish consisting of Swiss cheeses melted with white wine and served with bread cubes for dipping.

B. True/False: Egg and Breakfast Review

T F **1.** Fresh or high-grade raw eggs are firmer (less runny) than old or low-grade eggs.

T F **2.** The highest U.S.D.A. grade for fresh eggs is grade A.

T F **3.** One extra-large shell egg weighs slightly more than 2 oz (including the shell).

T F **4.** Egg yolks are high in fat.

T F **5.** The green color sometimes seen in eggs is due to overcooking.

T F **6.** A custard mixture must be heated to the boiling point of water (212°F/100°C) so that it will set properly.

T F **7.** Egg whites whip better and make a richer foam if the bowl is lightly greased before breaking the eggs into it.

T F **8.** Hard-cooked eggs will be tough and rubbery unless they are cooked long enough to be tenderized.

T F **9.** To make soft-cooked eggs, shell eggs are boiled for 5 to 7 minutes.

T F **10.** The air sac is located at the small end of the egg.

T F **11.** A pinch of cream of tartar improves the foaming ability of egg whites.

T F **12.** Making a true French omelet requires high heat.

T F **13.** A standard spinach soufflé is made from a thick white sauce, egg yolks, chopped cooked spinach (and sometimes other ingredients for flavoring), plus whipped egg whites folded in just before baking.

T F **14.** Waffle batter is usually thinner than pancake batter.

T F **15.** Pancake batter should be beaten well to develop a smooth texture.

T F **16.** The best way to prepare a large quantity of bacon is to cook it in the deep-fryer.

T F **17.** A pound of ground coffee makes approximately 4 gallons of brewed coffee.

Dairy and Cheese Review I

1. In the blanks provided, write in the name of the milk or cream products described.

(a) _____ Fresh, liquid, skim milk that has been cultured by bacteria.

(b) _____ Milk that has had about 60% of its water content removed.

(c) _____ Skim milk that has been dried to a powder.

(d) _____ Milk produced by disease-free herds under strict sanitary conditions.

(e) _____ Milk that has not been pasteurized.

(f) _____ Cream that has been fermented by certain bacteria to make it thick.

(g) _____ Sweetened milk with more than half its moisture removed.

(h) _____ Milk with all or nearly all its fat removed.

(i) _____ Milk with added vitamins.

2. In the blanks provided, write in the fat content (in percent) of each of the following milk and cream products.

(a) _____% Heavy whipping cream

(b) _____% Whole milk

(c) _____% Half-and-half

(d) _____% Skim milk

(e) _____% Butter

(f) _____% Light cream

3. What is yogurt? _____

_____

4. Name four conditions or substances that can make milk curdle.

(a) _____

(b) _____

(c) _____

(d) _____

5. In order to be in the best condition for whipping, heavy cream should be at about what temperature?

_____

6. Describe the appearance of properly whipped cream. What happens if the cream is whipped too much?

_____

_____

_____

7. What is the highest U.S.D.A. grade of butter? _____

8. What does the term "ripen" mean when referring to cheese?

_____

_____

_____

9. Cheeses can be classified according to how and if they are ripened. List the five categories, and give an example of each kind of cheese.

(a) _____ Example: _____

(b) _____ Example: _____

(c) _____ Example: _____

(d) _____ Example: _____

(e) _____ Example: _____

10. The label on a package of soft cheese indicates a net weight of 8 oz (227 g) and a fat content of 75%. What is the total weight of the fat in the cheese? Explain your answer. (Caution: This may be a trick question.)

_____

_____

_____

11. What is the proper serving temperature for most cheeses?

_____

D. Cheese Review II

The left column below lists the names of various cheeses. The column on the right lists various categories or kinds of cheese. In the space before the name of each cheese, write the letter corresponding to the kind of cheese it is.

_____ 1. Cheddar

_____ 2. Roquefort

_____ 3. Boucheron

_____ 4. Brie

_____ 5. Limburger

_____ 6. Parmesan

_____ 7. Emmenthaler

_____ 8. American

_____ 9. Stilton

_____ 10. Port Salut

_____ 11. Mozzarella

_____ 12. Gorgonzola

_____ 13. Romano

_____ 14. Fontina

_____ 15. Ricotta

_____ 16. Liederkranz

_____ 17. Cottage

_____ 18. Camembert

_____ 19. Bel Paese

_____ 20. Montrachet

a. Unripened

b. Semisoft

c. Soft ripened

d. Hard ripened

e. Blue-veined

f. Goat cheese

g. Hard grating (grana)

h. Process

E. Recipe Conversion

The following ingredients and quantities are for a Welsh Rabbit recipe that yields 25 portions at 4 oz each. Convert the recipe to the yields indicated.

	25 portions, 4 oz each	4 portions, 4 oz each	16 portions, 3 oz each
Worcestershire sauce	3 tbsp	_____	_____
Dry mustard	2 tsp	_____	_____
Cayenne	pinch	_____	_____
Beer	2½ cups	_____	_____
Cheddar cheese	5 lb	_____	_____
White bread*	25 slices	_____	_____

Note: This ingredient is calculated differently from the others.

Recipe Conversion—Metric

The following ingredients and quantities are for a Welsh Rabbit recipe that yields 25 portions at 125 g each. Convert the recipe to the yields indicated.

	25 portions, 125 g each	4 portions, 125 g each	16 portions, 100 g each
Worcestershire sauce	45 mL	_____	_____
Dry mustard	10 mL	_____	_____
Cayenne	pinch	_____	_____
Beer	625 mL	_____	_____
Cheddar cheese	2.5 kg	_____	_____
White bread*	25 slices	_____	_____

Note: This ingredient is calculated differently from the others.

F. Portion Cost

Cost out the following recipe. For prices of the ingredients, use figures supplied by your instructor or the *Sample Prices* on pages 223–224.

ITEM: **CHEESE TART**

Ingredient	Recipe Quantity	AP Quantity	Price	Total Amount
Flour	2 lb	_____	_____	_____
Shortening	1 lb 4 oz	_____	_____	_____
Salt	1½ oz	_____	_____	_____
Water	8 oz	_____	_____	_____
Gruyère cheese	2 lb	_____	_____	_____
Eggs	24	_____	_____	_____
Heavy cream	1 qt	_____	_____	_____
Milk	2 qt	_____	_____	_____
Salt	½ oz	_____	_____	_____

Total cost _____

Number of portions 48

Cost per portion _____

Portion Cost—Metric

Cost out the following recipe. For prices of the ingredients, use figures supplied by your instructor or the *Sample Prices* on pages 223–224.

ITEM: **CHEESE TART**

Ingredient	Recipe Quantity	AP Quantity	Price	Total Amount
Flour	1 kg	_____	_____	_____
Shortening	625 g	_____	_____	_____
Salt	15 g	_____	_____	_____
Water	250 mL	_____	_____	_____
Gruyère cheese	1 kg	_____	_____	_____
Eggs	24	_____	_____	_____
Heavy cream	1 L	_____	_____	_____
Milk	2 L	_____	_____	_____
Salt	15 g	_____	_____	_____

Total cost		_____
Number of portions		48
Cost per portion		_____

FOOD PRESENTATION AND GARNISH

This chapter concerns itself with the appearance of food rather than with cooking techniques. The material is meant to be studied not for its own sake but for its application to the food preparations that you learn in the rest of your studies. While it may seem very theoretical at first, it has many practical uses.

After studying Chapter 22, you should be able to:

1. Explain the importance of attractive food presentation.

2. Serve food that is attractively arranged on the plate or platter, with proper balance of color, shape, and texture.

3. Identify common terms from classical garniture that are still in general use today.

4. Garnish a banquet platter with attractive and appropriate vegetable accompaniments.

5. Produce and use correctly a wide variety of simple garnishes.

6. Plan and arrange attractive food platters for buffets.

A. Terms

Fill in each blank with the term that is defined or described.

_____ **1.** To add an edible decorative item to food.

_____ **2.** A decorative edible item added to food.

_____ **3.** To trim mushroom caps with a grooved pattern.

_____ **4.** A type of buffet serving only appetizers, usually to accompany drinks.

_____ **5.** The centerpiece of a cold buffet platter.

_____ **6.** An oval relish dish.

_____ **7.** Bread slices cut into triangles or heart shapes, toasted, and used as garnish.

B. Garnish Review

In the blanks provided, write the specific food items or ingredients that the garnish terms refer to.

_____ **1.** Niçoise

_____ **2.** Dubarry

_____ **3.** Lyonnaise

_____ **4.** Parmentier

_____ **5.** Printanière

_____ **6.** Judic

_____ **7.** Primeurs

_____ **8.** Florentine

_____ **9.** Princesse

_____ **10.** Bouquetière

_____ **11.** Doria

_____ **12.** Jardinière

_____ **13.** Vichy

_____ **14.** Forestière

_____ **15.** Crécy

_____ **16.** Fermière

_____ **17.** Clamart

_____ **18.** Provençale

C. True / False

T   **F**   **1.** The main meat or fish item on a plate is always placed in the center.

T   **F**   **2.** The term garnish sometimes refers to vegetable accompaniments.

T   **F**   **3.** A T-bone steak should be plated so that the bone is toward the back of the plate, away from the customer.

T   **F**   **4.** To make the portions look generous, the meat and vegetable items on a plate should be piled up against each other.

T   **F**   **5.** Every buffet platter requires a centerpiece.

T   **F**   **6.** Filet mignon plated with various garnishes is listed on the menu as "filet mignon with garni."

T   **F**   **7.** A simple garnish should always be edible, even if it is not intended to be eaten.

T   **F**   **8.** Deep-fried foods are usually not suited for chafing-dish service.

T   **F**   **9.** On a buffet, sauces and dressings should be placed next to the items with which they are to be eaten.

D. Review of Cold Platter Design

Following the principles outlined on pages 601–603 of the text, draw diagrams of food arrangements on each of the four platters outlined below. Develop your own designs; do not copy the examples in Figure 22.9. In the blanks provided, you may indicate what foods you are using. Use your ideas, or whatever food items are assigned by your instructor. (A platter may have more than one main food item and / or more than one garnish; for example, slices of veal pâté and slices of pickled veal tongue as two main items on one platter.)

Centerpiece _____

Main item(s) _____

_____

Garnish(es) _____

_____

Centerpiece _____

Main item(s) _____

_____

Garnish(es) _____

_____

Centerpiece _____

Main item(s) _____

_____

Garnish(es) _____

_____

Centerpiece _____

Main item(s) _____

_____

Garnish(es) _____

_____

BAKESHOP PRODUCTION: BASIC PRINCIPLES AND INGREDIENTS

This is the first of seven chapters dealing with the bakeshop. We begin with some basic principles and an introduction to the primary ingredients used in baking. You will need to understand this material before proceeding to the production chapters.

After studying Chapter 24, you should be able to:

1. Explain the importance of weighing baking ingredients.

2. Use a baker's balance scale.

3. Use formulas based on baker's percentages.

4. Explain the factors that control the development of gluten in baked products.

5. Explain the changes that take place in a dough or batter as it bakes.

6. Prevent or retard the staling of baked items.

7. Discuss the major ingredients of baked goods and their functions and characteristics.

A. Terms

Fill in each blank with the term that is defined or described.

_____ 1. The chemical name for regular refined sugar or table sugar.

_____ 2. A flavoring ingredient consisting of flavorful oils mixed with water with the aid of vegetable gums or other substances.

_____ 3. A substance, made up of proteins present in wheat flour, that gives structure and strength to baked goods.

_____ 4. Flour with a high protein content, derived from hard wheat.

_____ 5. Flour with a low protein content, from soft wheat.

_____ 6. The process by which yeast changes carbohydrates to alcohol and carbon dioxide gas.

_____ 7. The primary sugar present in corn syrup.

_____ 8. The rendered fat of hogs.

_____ 9. The change in texture of baked goods due in part to the loss of moisture by the starch granules.

_____ 10. A flavoring ingredient consisting of flavorful oils and other substances dissolved in alcohol.

_____ 11. The product that results when cocoa beans are roasted and ground.

_____ 12. The white or yellowish fat that is a component of the product described in number 11.

_____ 13. The dry powder that remains after part of the fat is removed from the product described in number 11.

_____ 14. The dried powder as described in number 13, but processed with alkali.

_____ 15. The product that is made when sugar is added to the product described in number 11.

_____ 16. The product that is made when sugar and milk solids are added to the product described in number 11.

_____ 17. The production or incorporation of gases in a baked product to increase volume and to produce shape and texture.

_____ 18. Any of a group of solid fats, usually white and tasteless, that have been especially formulated for baking.

_____ 19. The process of beating fat and sugar together to incorporate air.

_____ 20. The process of whipping eggs, with or without sugar, to incorporate air.

_____ 21. The finest or smoothest variety of confectioners' sugar.

B. Flour Review

Flour is the fundamental raw material of the bakeshop. Define or describe, as thoroughly as you can, each of the following products. If the product is a wheat flour, be sure to indicate whether it is a strong (high-gluten) flour or weak (low-gluten) flour.

1. Cake flour: _____

_____

_____

2. Bread flour: _____

_____

_____

3. Pastry flour: _____

_____

_____

4. Rye flour: _____

_____

_____

5. Pumpernickel: _____

_____

_____

6. Rye meal: _____

_____

_____

7. Patent flour: _____

_____

_____

8. Pastry flour: _____

_____

_____

9. Whole wheat flour: _____

_____

_____

10. Bran flour: _____

_____

_____

11. Rye blend: _____

_____

_____

C. Short-Answer Questions

1. What is the weight of 1 pint of water? _____

2. What other liquid ingredients, commonly used in the bakeshop, weigh the same as water? _____

_____

3. List four factors that influence the development of gluten in doughs and batters.

(a) _____

(b) _____

(c) _____

(d) _____

4. Fresh-baked goods can often become stale quickly. What are three factors that can help slow down the staling process?

(a) _____

(b) _____

(c) _____

5. List five functions of fats in baked goods.

(a) _____

(b) _____

(c) _____

(d) _____

(e) _____

6. List five functions of sugars in baked goods.

(a) _____

(b) _____

(c) _____

(d) _____

(e) _____

7. List eight functions of eggs in baked goods.

(a) _____

(b) _____

(c) _____

(d) _____

(e) _____

(f) _____

(g) _____

(h) _____

8. At what temperatures does yeast grow best? _____

At what temperature is yeast killed? _____

9. What are three functions of salt in baked goods?

(a) _____

(b) _____

(c) _____

D. Using Baker's Percentages

Use the percentages given to calculate the quantities needed in the following formulas. If you normally work with U.S. units of measure, fill in the blanks to the left of the percent column. If you normally work with metric units, fill in the blanks to the right of the percent column. You are provided with either the weight of flour or the total yield by weight.

	U.S.	Percent	Metric
I.			
Butter	_____	80%	_____
Sugar	_____	60%	_____
Salt	_____	1%	_____
Ground almonds	_____	50%	_____
Eggs	_____	16.5%	_____
Pastry flour	5 lb	100%	2500 g
II.			
Butter	_____	90%	_____
Sugar	_____	100%	_____
Sweet chocolate	_____	135%	_____
Egg yolks	_____	100%	_____
Egg whites	_____	150%	_____
Sugar	_____	75%	_____
Cake flour	_____	100%	_____
Yield	2 lb 5.5 oz	750%	1125 g

III.

Pastry flour	3 lb	100%	1500 g
Baking powder		5%	
Baking soda		1.25%	
Salt		1.25%	
Sugar		6.5%	
Butter		10%	
Raisins		20%	
Buttermilk		90%	

YEAST PRODUCTS

Bread is perhaps the most important product of the bakeshop. Procedures for making breads and other yeast products are discussed in Chapter 25. To make these products successfully, you must understand how to mix ingredients into doughs, how to control gluten development, and how to control yeast fermentation.

After studying Chapter 25, you should be able to:

1. Produce breads and dinner rolls.

2. Produce sweet dough products.

3. Product Danish pastry and croissants.

A. Terms

Fill in each blank with the term that is defined or described.

_____ 1. The process by which yeast acts on carbohydrates to produce alcohol and carbon dioxide gas.

_____ 2. The continuation of the yeast action after the dough is shaped into loaves or other products, resulting in increase in volume.

_____ 3. A dough that is low in fat and sugar.

_____ 4. A dough that is high in fat and sugar, and sometimes eggs.

_____ 5. The rapid rising of a yeast dough in the oven due to production and expansion of gases.

_____ 6. A dough in which fat is incorporated into the dough in many layers by using a folding and rolling procedure.

_____ **7.** A yeast dough mixing method in which all ingredients are combined at once.

_____ **8.** A dough that has fermented too long.

_____ **9.** A dough that has not fermented long enough.

_____ **10.** A method of deflating dough to expel carbon dioxide.

_____ **11.** The process of shaping scaled dough into smooth, round balls.

_____ **12.** A crescent-shaped roll made of a rolled-in dough.

_____ **13.** Crumb topping for pastries, made of flour, butter, and sugar.

B. True/False

T   F   **1.** The dough arm attachment is used for mixing most yeast doughs.

T   F   **2.** A well-developed French bread dough should be quite sticky.

T   F   **3.** Club rolls and Parker House rolls are two examples of rolled-in dough products.

T   F   **4.** Punching is done by hitting the dough with your fist.

T   F   **5.** The temperature of a proof box should be set at 75°F (24°C) for most yeast products.

T   F   **6.** When made-up bread loaves are placed in baking pans, seams should be on the bottom.

T   F   **7.** Most breads and rolls are baked at a temperature of about 350°F (175°C).

T   F   **8.** Rich doughs are usually slightly underfermented before punching.

T   F   **9.** Bread in the oven is tested for doneness by testing it with a dough thermometer.

T   F   **10.** To maintain freshness, bread should be stored in the refrigerator.

C. Mixing Yeast Doughs

1. In the space below, write the procedure for mixing yeast doughs by the straight dough method.

2. In the space below, write the procedure for mixing rich yeast doughs by the modified straight dough method.

3. In the space below, write the procedure for mixing yeast doughs by the sponge method.

D. Using Baker's Percentages

Use the percentages given to calculate the quantities needed in the following formula. If you normally work with U.S. units of measure, fill in the blanks to the left of the percent column. If you normally work with metric units, fill in the blanks to the right of the percent column.

	U.S.	Percent	Metric
Milk		30%	
Yeast		5%	
Bread flour	6 oz	30%	175 g
Butter		40%	
Sugar		20%	
Salt		1.25%	
Eggs		35%	
Bread flour	14 oz	70%	425 g
Raisins		12.5%	

CHAPTER 26

QUICK BREADS

This chapter deals with products that are not only very popular but also very easy to make. Consequently, this will be useful information to you in your career, so you should study it well.

After studying Chapter 26, you should be able to:

1. Prepare baking powder biscuits and variations.
2. Prepare muffins, loaf breads, coffee cakes, and corn breads.
3. Prepare popovers.

A. Terms

Fill in each blank with the term that is defined or described.

_____ 1. The development of elongated holes inside muffin products.

_____ 2. A batter that is liquid enough to be poured.

_____ 3. A batter that is too thick to be poured, but that will drop from a spoon in lumps.

_____ 4. A baked product made of a thin batter, leavened only by steam, and characterized by very large holes on the inside.

B. Review of Mixing Methods

1. In the space below, write the procedure for mixing doughs by the biscuit method.

2. In the space below, write the procedure for mixing batters by the muffin method.

C. Using Baker's Percentages

Use the percentages given to calculate the quantities needed in the following formula. If you normally work with U.S. units of measure, fill in the blanks to the left of the percent column. If you normally work with metric units, fill in the blanks to the right of the percent column.

	U.S.	Percent	Metric
Pastry flour	_____	100%	_____
Sugar	_____	40%	_____
Baking powder	_____	5%	_____
Baking soda	_____	0.6%	_____
Salt	_____	1.25%	_____
Walnuts	_____	25%	_____
Eggs	_____	40%	_____
Banana pulp	_____	90%	_____
Melted butter	_____	33%	_____
Yield	7 lb 8 oz	334%	3348 g

CAKES AND ICINGS

Because cakes are such delicate products, mixing and baking them requires a great deal of precision and care. It is important, then, that you study and review this chapter thoroughly in order to make superior cakes.

After studying Chapter 27, you should be able to:

1. Perform basic cake mixing methods.
2. Understand the characteristics of basic cake types.
3. Produce both high-fat or shortened cakes and low-fat or foam-type cakes.
4. Prepare basic icings.
5. Assemble and ice cakes.

A. Terms

Fill in each blank with the term that is defined or described.

_____ 1. A type of cake based on an egg-white foam and containing no fat.

_____ 2. A type of cake made with an egg-white foam and oil.

_____ 3. A classic cake made of equal parts butter, sugar, flour, and eggs.

_____ 4. A classic sponge cake made of eggs, sugar, flour, and melted butter, but with no other liquid.

_____ 5. An icing made by creaming together fat and sugar.

_____ 6. An icing made by mixing confectioners' sugar and egg whites.

_____ **7.** An icing that consists of a sugar syrup that has been crystallized to a smooth, creamy white mass.

_____ **8.** An icing that consists primarily of confectioners' sugar mixed with water.

_____ **9.** A glossy, transparent coating that gives a shine to baked products.

B. Review of Cake Mixing Methods

1. In the space below, explain how to mix cakes by the creaming method. Be sure to include all the necessary steps, and number the steps.

2. In the space below, explain how to mix cakes by the two-stage method. Be sure to include all the necessary steps, and number the steps.

3. In the space below, explain how to mix angel food cakes. Be sure to include all the necessary steps, and number the steps.

4. In the space below, explain how to mix genoise-type sponge cakes. Include all the necessary steps, and number the steps.

5. In the space below, explain how to mix chiffon cakes. Write the procedure in the form of numbered steps.

C. Review of Icing Preparations

1. Fondant must be warmed for use, but it should not be heated above 100°F (38°C). Why? _____

   _____

2. How do you make chocolate fondant? _____

   _____

3. Name and describe the three main types of buttercream.

   (a) _____

   _____

   (b) _____

   _____

   (c) _____

   _____

4. What is decorator's buttercream? _____

   _____

   _____

5. What is royal icing used for? _____

6. Briefly describe how to make and how to store royal icing.

   _____

   _____

   _____

   _____

7. Briefly describe two methods for icing cupcakes.

   (a) _____

   _____

   (b) _____

   _____

8. Flat icings are handled and applied in the same way as what other type of icing? _____

_____

9. What is a foam icing? _____

_____

D. Using Baker's Percentages

Use the percentages given to calculate the quantities needed in the following formula. If you normally work with U.S. units of measure, fill in the blanks to the left of the percent column. If you normally work with metric units, fill in the blanks to the right of the percent column.

	U.S.	Percent	Metric
Flour	_____	100%	_____
Salt	_____	2%	_____
Baking powder	_____	2%	_____
Emulsified shortening	_____	67%	_____
Sugar	_____	117%	_____
Nonfat milk solids	_____	6%	_____
Water	_____	45%	_____
Eggs	_____	67%	_____
Raisins	_____	25%	_____
Yield	8 lb 8 oz	430%	3865 g

COOKIES

Like most kitchen and bakeshop tasks, learning to make cookies easily and efficiently is primarily a matter of developing manual skills. But like most food service tasks, it also requires some understanding of theory and basic principles. This chapter will help you review those principles.

After studying Chapter 28, you should be able to:

1. Understand the causes of crispness, softness, chewiness, and spread in cookies.
2. Prepare cookie doughs by the three basic mixing methods.
3. Prepare seven basic types of cookies: dropped, bagged, rolled, molded, icebox, bar, and sheet.
4. Bake and cool cookies properly.

A. Terms

Fill in each blank with the term that is defined or described.

_____ 1. Readily absorbing moisture.

_____ 2. A cookie made of coconut mixed with meringue.

_____ 3. A rich, rather crumbly Scottish cookie made of butter, flour, and sugar; some variations also contain egg.

_____ 4. Finger-shaped soft cookies made from a sponge batter.

The following terms refer to categories of cookies based on makeup method.

_____ **5.** Cookies cut from refrigerated, sausage-shaped pieces of dough.

_____ **6.** Cookies pressed from a pastry bag.

_____ **7.** Cookies made with a cookie cutter.

_____ **8.** Cookies made by spreading dough or batter in sheet pans, baking, and then cutting out squares or rectangles.

_____ **9.** Cookies made from lumps of dough dropped onto baking pans.

_____ **10.** Cookies made from cylinders of dough flattened onto sheet pans, baked, then cut crosswise into pieces.

_____ **11.** Cookies made from equal pieces of dough cut from a cylinder, placed on sheet pans, then pressed flat.

B. Review of Cookie Mixing Methods

1. Using numbered steps, describe the creaming method for mixing cookies.

2. Using numbered steps, describe the one-stage method for mixing cookies.

C. Short-Answer Questions

1. A cookie dough is more likely to spread when baked if its content of granulated sugar is _____ .

2. The main reason for shaping cookies uniformly during makeup is _____ .

3. Cookie dough to be rolled out with a rolling pin should be at what temperature? _____

4. What is likely to happen to cookies baked at too high a temperature? _____

5. What should be done with freshly baked cookies before they are put in containers for storage? _____

_____

6. How much flour should be used for dusting when rolling out cookie dough with a rolling pin? _____

_____

7. What is the main indication of doneness when cookies are baked? _____

8. If a rich cookie dough burns too easily when baked, what can be done to prevent burning? _____

_____

D. Using Baker's Percentages

Use the percentages given to calculate the quantities needed in the following formula. If you normally work with U.S. units of measure, fill in the blanks to the left of the percent column. If you normally work with metric units, fill in the blanks to the right of the percent column.

	U.S.	Percent	Metric
Butter		67%	
Brown sugar		133%	
Salt		1.5%	
Eggs		33%	
Vanilla		3%	
Milk		8%	
Pastry flour	1 lb 14 oz	100%	900 g
Baking powder		4%	
Baking soda		2%	
Rolled oats		83%	
Raisins		50%	

PIES AND PASTRY

Many kinds of products are presented in Chapter 29, and the techniques used to prepare them are important ones. The various review exercises here will help you study the various procedures involved in pastry making.

After studying Chapter 29, you should be able to:

1. Prepare flaky and mealy pie doughs.
2. Prepare crumb crusts and short or cookie crusts.
3. Assemble and bake pies.
4. Prepare pie fillings.
5. Prepare puff pastry dough and puff dough products.
6. Prepare eclair paste and eclair paste products.
7. Prepare standard meringues and meringue desserts.
8. Prepare fruit desserts.

A. Terms

Fill in each blank with the term that is defined or described.

_____ 1. A type of dough that is mixed like pie dough but rolled and folded like puff paste.

_____ 2. A dessert consisting of ice cream covered with meringue and browned in the oven.

_____ 3. Starch that thickens liquids without cooking, because it has been precooked.

_____ 4. A dessert made of layers of puff pastry alternating with layers of pastry cream or other cream.

_____ **5.** French name for eclair paste.

_____ **6.** A type of meringue made with boiling syrup.

_____ **7.** Tiny cream puffs, often filled with ice cream and served with chocolate syrup.

_____ **8.** A type of meringue made with a warmed mixture of egg whites and sugar.

_____ **9.** A type of pie filling that is lightened by the addition of whipped egg whites.

_____ **10.** A starch that makes a clear gel when cooked and that does not break down when frozen.

_____ **11.** A crisp disk of baked meringue containing nuts.

_____ **12.** A baked dessert made of sliced, sugared apples topped with a crumb or streussel topping flavored with cinnamon.

_____ **13.** A baked meringue shell filled with ice cream.

B. Pie Review

1. The main types of pie dough are _____ and _____ .

2. The difference between the two main types of pie dough mostly depends on _____

_____ .

3. Water for pie dough should be at what temperature? _____

4. What are two functions of salt in pie dough? _____

_____

_____

5. If shortening is used to make pie dough, what type of shortening is the correct one to use? _____

_____

6. A basic graham cracker crust is made with what ingredients?

_____

7. Assume you have made a fruit pie filling by the cooked juice method. At about what temperature should the

filling be when the pie shell is filled? _____

8. Vanilla cream pie filling is thickened with _____ .

9. The best thickening agent to use for fruit pie fillings is _____ .

10. To prevent lumping, starch must be mixed with _____ or with _____ before being added to a hot liquid.

11. In the space below, list the four ingredients in basic pie dough, then write the procedure for mixing the ingredients to make a dough. Use numbered steps. Be sure to explain the difference between the two main types of dough.

     Ingredients: _____

                  _____

                  _____

                  _____

     Procedure:

12. In the space below, explain how to make fruit pie fillings using the cooked juice method. Write the procedure in the form of numbered steps.

13. In the space below, explain how to make fruit pie fillings using the cooked fruit method. Write the procedure in the form of numbered steps.

C. True/False

T F **1.** Eclair paste is made with pastry flour.

T F **2.** Puff paste is rolled and folded with the same number of folds as Danish pastry.

T F **3.** Puff pastry is leavened with baking powder.

T F **4.** Eclair paste is leavened with baking soda.

T F **5.** Puff paste is refrigerated briefly between turns, especially if the bakeshop is warm.

T F **6.** Butter to be rolled into puff paste must be well chilled and hard so that it won't ooze out of the dough.

T F **7.** A 4-fold gets its name because it results in four times as many layers in the dough each time it is done.

T F **8.** Eclairs are baked at a low temperature to give them time to puff up.

T F **9.** The flour mixture for eclair paste is chilled before the eggs are added.

T F **10.** Hard meringues are baked at a low temperature so that they will dry out but will not brown.

T F **11.** Meringue pie topping is made with about 4 oz of sugar per pound of egg whites (250 g sugar per kilogram of egg whites).

D. Using Baker's Percentages

Use the percentages given to calculate the quantities needed in the following formulas. If you normally work with U.S. units of measure, fill in the blanks to the left of the percent column. If you normally work with metric units, fill in the blanks to the right of the percent column. You are provided with either the weight of flour or the total yield by weight.

	U.S.	Percent	Metric
I.			
Pastry flour	_____	100%	_____
Shortening	_____	70%	_____
Salt	_____	2%	_____
Water	_____	30%	_____
Yield	____14 lb____	202%	____6000 g____

II.

Pastry flour	4 lb	100%	2000 g
Sugar	_____	17%	_____
Butter	_____	50%	_____
Egg yolks	_____	8%	_____
Water	_____	25%	_____
Salt	_____	1%	_____

CREAMS, CUSTARDS, PUDDINGS, FROZEN DESSERTS, AND SAUCES

Like the previous chapter, this chapter presents a wide variety of techniques and products. Some of these products, like pastry cream, are used as components of many different kinds of desserts and pastries, so it is important to know them well. Since many of the recipes are based on egg custards, it will also help you to review what you learned about eggs in Chapter 21.

After studying Chapter 30, you should be able to:

1. Cook sugar syrups to various stages of hardness.
2. Prepare vanilla custard sauce, pastry cream, and baked custard.
3. Prepare starch-thickened puddings and baked puddings.
4. Prepare bavarians, chiffons, mousses, and dessert soufflés.
5. Assemble frozen desserts.
6. Prepare dessert sauces.

A. Terms

Fill in each blank with the term that is defined or described.

_____ 1. French term for vanilla custard sauce.

_____ 2. A flavored simple syrup, used to moisten and flavor some cakes.

_____ 3. A thick stirred custard thickened with starch as well as with eggs; used as a pastry and pie filling and as a pudding.

_____ 4. A baked custard made in a caramel-lined mold, so that it has a caramel topping when turned out of the mold.

_____ 5. A white cornstarch pudding, often flavored with almond extract.

_____ 6. A pudding similar to a cornstarch pudding but also containing eggs.

_____ 7. A dessert consisting of alternating layers of ice cream and fruit or syrup in a tall, narrow glass.

_____ 8. Ice cream containing no eggs.

_____ 9. The increase in volume of ice cream during freezing due to incorporation of air.

_____ 10. A chilled dessert made of flavored custard sauce, gelatin, and whipped cream.

_____ 11. A soft or creamy dessert made light or fluffy by the addition of whipped cream or whipped egg whites or both.

_____ 12. A dessert consisting of one or two scoops of ice cream or sherbet in a dish or glass, topped with any of a number of syrups, fruits, or toppings.

_____ 13. A molded ice cream dessert consisting of two or more layers of different ice creams.

_____ 14. A baked, pudding-like dessert lightened with whipped egg whites.

_____ 15. A frozen dessert similar to ice cream but with a lower butterfat content.

_____ 16. A dessert consisting of a pear half, chocolate sauce, and toasted almonds on top of vanilla ice cream.

_____ 17. A frozen dessert made of fruit juices, water, sugar, and sometimes egg whites, but containing no milk products.

_____ 18. A frozen dessert similar to the one described in number 17, but with a coarse, crystalline texture, and made without egg whites.

_____ 19. A dessert or pie filling containing gelatin and whipped egg whites.

_____ 20. A dessert consisting of a peach half and raspberry sauce on top of vanilla ice cream.

_____ 21. The browning of sugar caused by heat.

B. Review of Sugar Cooking

1. A simple syrup is a solution of equal parts _____ and_____ .

2. Dessert syrup is a simple syrup plus _____ .

3. When a syrup is boiled, moisture gradually evaporates, and the temperature of the syrup gradually _____ .

4. If a syrup is cooked to 300°F (150°C) and then cooled, its texture will be _____ .

5. If a syrup is cooked until it turns light brown, the resulting product is called _____ .

6. If an acid, such as _____ , is added to a syrup before cooking, some of the sugar turns

   to _____ . The advantage of this is _____

   _____ .

7. When you want to cook a syrup to a certain stage of doneness, the tool you need to accurately test for doneness

   is _____ .

8. When the instructions in a candy recipe say to "wash down the sides of the pan with a brush dipped in water,"

   the purpose of this direction is _____

   _____ .

C. Review of Basic Custards and Creams

1. The basic ingredients of vanilla custard sauce are _____ , _____ ,

   _____ , and vanilla.

2. Vanilla custard sauce is completely cooked when it reaches a temperature of _____ .

3. Why is a double boiler generally used to make vanilla custard sauce? _____

   _____

4. Why is it important to use clean, sanitary equipment when making vanilla custard sauce and pastry cream?

_____

_____

5. Why is it important to chill pastry cream quickly after it is cooked? _____

_____

6. After pastry cream is cooked, it is poured into _____ pans so that it will cool quickly.

7. What is the advantage of baking custards in a hot-water bath? _____

_____

8. When making baked custards, what is the advantage of scalding the milk before adding it to the eggs?

_____

_____

9. In the space below, write the procedure for preparing vanilla custard sauce. Use numbered steps.

10. In the space that follows, write the procedure for preparing vanilla pastry cream.

D. True/False

T   F   **1.** Lemon pie filling is made using the same technique as vanilla pastry cream.

T   F   **2.** A boiling syrup that is at the crack stage is hotter than a boiling syrup at the hard ball stage.

T   F   **3.** Corn syrup should not be added to a boiling sugar syrup because it may cause crystallization.

T   F   **4.** French-style ice cream contains egg yolks.

T   F   **5.** For sanitary reasons, vanilla custard sauce should be brought to a boil to kill bacteria.

T   F   **6.** When scalded milk is added to egg yolks, it should be added all at once.

T   F   **7.** A dessert soufflé is always baked at a low temperature (about 300°F/150°C) to give the soufflé time to rise properly.

T   F   **8.** If both whipped cream and whipped egg whites must be added to a chocolate mousse, the whipped cream is always added first.

T   F   **9.** If egg whites for a dessert soufflé are beaten with some sugar, this helps to make the soufflé more stable.

T   F   **10.** Butterscotch pudding is made by making vanilla pudding with extra butter, and adding scotch flavoring.

T   F   **11.** Frozen mousses can be still-frozen (not churn-frozen in an ice cream freezer) because they contain whipped cream or whipped egg whites.

T   F   **12.** A coupe is basically the same as a sundae.

E. Portion Cost

Cost out the following recipe. For prices of the ingredients, use figures supplied by your instructor or the *Sample Prices* on pages 223–224.

ITEM: **CHOCOLATE CREAM PIE**

Ingredient	Recipe Quantity	AP Quantity	Price	Total Amount
Flour	12 oz	_____	_____	_____
Shortening	8 oz	_____	_____	_____
Water	4 oz	_____	_____	_____
Milk	2 qt	_____	_____	_____
Sugar	1 lb	_____	_____	_____
Eggs	8	_____	_____	_____
Cornstarch	5 oz	_____	_____	_____
Sweet chocolate	4 oz	_____	_____	_____
Bitter chocolate	4 oz	_____	_____	_____
Butter	4 oz	_____	_____	_____
Vanilla	1 oz	_____	_____	_____

Total cost _____

Number of portions   24

Cost per portion _____

Portion Cost—Metric

Cost out the following recipe. For prices of the ingredients, use figures supplied by your instructor or the *Sample Prices* on pages 223–224.

ITEM: **CHOCOLATE CREAM PIE**

Ingredient	Recipe Quantity	AP Quantity	Price	Total Amount
Flour	375 g	_____	_____	_____
Shortening	250 g	_____	_____	_____
Water	125 g	_____	_____	_____
Milk	2 L	_____	_____	_____
Sugar	500 g	_____	_____	_____
Eggs	8	_____	_____	_____
Cornstarch	150 g	_____	_____	_____
Sweet chocolate	125 g	_____	_____	_____
Bitter chocolate	125 g	_____	_____	_____
Butter	125 g	_____	_____	_____
Vanilla	30 mL	_____	_____	_____

Total cost _____

Number of portions 24

Cost per portion _____

SAMPLE PRICES

Your instructors may want you to use the prices on current invoices when you do the Portion Cost exercises in this manual. If not, you may use the following hypothetical prices. Do not worry about whether or not these prices seem realistic. Prices change, but you can still practice the calculations with these numbers.

Meat, Poultry, and Fish

Beef brisket	$ 1.80 per lb	$ 3.89 per kg
Beef, ground	1.39 per lb	3.19 per kg
Chicken parts	0.85 per lb	1.85 per kg
Italian pork sausages	1.49 per lb	3.29 per kg
Sole fillets	5.99 per lb	13.00 per kg

Produce and Frozen Vegetables

Artichokes	$ 0.45 each	$ 0.45 each
Cabbage	0.25 per lb	0.55 per kg
Carrots	0.30 per lb	0.65 per kg
Leeks	1.10 per lb	2.40 per kg
Lemons	0.20 each	0.20 each
Lettuce, iceberg	0.80 per head	0.80 per head
Mushrooms	1.25 per lb	2.75 per kg
Onions, yellow	0.30 per lb	0.65 per kg
Peas, frozen	2.20 per 2½ lb pack	1.95 per kg
Peppers, green bell	0.50 per lb	1.15 per kg
Peppers, red bell	2.49 per lb	5.49 per kg
Peppers, Italian	0.80 per lb	1.75 per kg
Potatoes, all-purpose	0.20 per lb	0.45 per kg
Potatoes, baking, "100's" (8-oz average weight)	0.30 per lb	0.65 per kg
Shallots	1.50 per lb	3.50 per kg
Squash, butternut	0.35 per lb	0.75 per kg
Tomatoes	0.50 per lb	1.20 per kg

Dairy and Eggs

Butter	$ 1.70 per lb	$ 3.75 per kg
Milk	0.45 per qt	0.45 per L
Heavy cream	2.69 per qt	2.69 per L
Sour cream	1.09 per lb	2.40 per kg
Cheese, Gruyère	4.00 per lb	8.50 per kg
Cheese, Parmesan	6.00 per lb	13.00 per kg
Eggs, large	0.89 per dozen	0.89 per dozen

Groceries

Beets, canned	$ 0.60 per #2½ can	$ 0.60 per #2½ can
Breadcrumbs, dry	0.79 per lb	1.79 per kg
Chili powder	0.75 per oz	2.70 per 100 g
Chocolate, bitter	3.98 per lb	8.79 per kg
Chocolate, sweet	3.69 per lb	8.19 per kg
Cornstarch	0.59 per lb	1.29 per kg
Flour	0.15 per lb	0.35 per kg
Ginger, ground	1.40 per oz	5.00 per 100 g
Mayonnaise	6.50 per gal	1.65 per L
Oil, olive	3.29 per qt	3.29 per L
Oil, salad/vegetable	4.60 per gal	1.20 per L
Pepper, black	0.45 per oz	1.59 per 100 g
Raisins	1.09 per lb	2.39 per kg
Salt	0.15 per lb	0.35 per kg
Shortening	0.55 per lb	1.20 per kg
Soy sauce	1.25 per pt	2.50 per L
Spaghetti	0.79 per lb	1.75 per kg
Sugar, brown	0.45 per lb	1.00 per kg
Sugar, granulated	0.30 per lb	0.65 per kg
Tomato paste	0.70 per 1-lb can	0.75 per 500-g can
Tomato purée	0.45 per 1-lb can	0.50 per 500-g can
Tomatoes, whole, canned	0.35 per lb	0.75 per kg
Tomatoes, #10 can	2.10 per can	2.10 per can
Vanilla	10.00 per qt	10.00 per L
Vinegar, red wine	0.75 per qt	0.75 per L

Miscellaneous

Beef stock	$ 0.30 per qt	$ 0.30 per L
Chicken stock	0.25 per qt	0.25 per L
Fish stock	0.50 per qt	0.50 per L
Sherry wine	7.00 per qt	7.00 per L